FIREMEN
AT WAR

NEIL WALLINGTON

FIREMEN AT WAR

THE WORK OF LONDON'S FIRE-FIGHTERS IN THE SECOND WORLD WAR

DAVID & CHARLES
Newton Abbot

British Library Cataloguing in Publication Data

Wallington, Neil
Firemen at war.
1. World War, 1939–1945—England—London
2. London—Fires and fire prevention
I. Title
628.9'25'09421   TH9539.L8

ISBN 0-7153-7964-X

First published 1981
Second impression 1990

Filmset in Monophoto Plantin
by Latimer Trend & Company Ltd, Plymouth
Printed in Great Britain
by BPCC Wheatons Ltd.

To the men of today's fire service, who face the same hazards and dangers as their predecessors did during the London blitz, flying bomb and rocket attacks of forty years ago.

I see the damage done by the enemy attacks; but I also see, side by side with the devastation and amid the ruins, quiet, confident, bright and smiling eyes, beaming with a consciousness of being associated with a cause far higher and wider than any human or personal issue. I see the spirit of an unconquerable people.

Winston Churchill,
12 April 1941

Contents

Author's Note

My interest in the part played by the London Fire Service on the home front during the last war has always been stimulated by the retired firemen I have met from time to time. On such occasions, these men would tell vivid tales of the blitz, flying bomb and rocket attacks, and of the holocaust that each had endured and survived.

As a fireman of a later generation, I can only begin to imagine what those war years were like. All firemen have at some time or other seen the destruction that fire can cause, and also been witness to much human tragedy. But it is not easy to appreciate how the relatively small numbers of the professional London Fire Brigade came together with thousands of volunteer and totally inexperienced auxiliaries, to tackle nightly infernos of a size never before faced by firemen. It is difficult to envisage such fire-fighting as took place, with at best an inadequate and uncertain supply of water, let alone the dangers to firemen from the falling and exploding bombs. Perhaps above all, neither I nor any of my present-day colleagues are likely to have suffered the extreme exhaustion that slowly overcame firemen during the blitz months.

That London was not razed to the ground during the last war is a direct tribute to the sacrifice and perseverance of its fire service. In this book I have attempted to portray some of the life and times of London's fire-fighters under wartime conditions. Wherever possible, the accounts and recollections of the men and women who formed London's fire defence have been left to tell their own story of this very dramatic period in the annals of the fire service.

9

The term 'London Fire Service' is the umbrella title that was given to the professional London Fire Brigade and the Auxiliary Fire Service of the London area formed in 1938.

AUTHOR'S NOTE TO THE REPRINTED FIRST EDITION

This reprint is in response to the continuing interest in fire-fighting and rescue during the London fire blitz and the later flying bomb and rocket attacks.

In its own way, I hope that the book will help to mark the 50th anniversary of the London blitz on 7 September 1990. Whilst there have been quite a number of commemorative histories recalling Dunkirk, the Battle of Britain and other significant events during the Second World War, the London fire-fighter's story is still not widely appreciated or remembered. These pages provide a graphic reminder of the demanding role and contribution of those who formed London's 'thin red line' of 1940–1945 and of battles fought out on the very streets of the capital.

Since the first edition, I have received very many letters and favourable comments from today's fire-fighters regarding the achievements of the crews of the London Fire Service as set out in *Firemen at War*. There is no doubt in my mind that such modern day professional appreciation fully reinforces the simple dedication at the beginning of this book.

Neil Wallington
Woodbury, Exeter, Devon.
April 1990

Introduction

The aerial bombardment of an enemy-held territory had its origins in the 1914–18 war, when primitive bombing raids were made on front-line positions both by Royal Flying Corps and by German aircraft. Early on in that terrible war, in April 1915, zeppelin airships dropped bombs over Dover, thus making the very first air-raid on the United Kingdom; this was almost certainly the first direct involvement in war of a civilian population at home, many miles from the carnage taking place across the Channel. Later that year, came a serious zeppelin incendiary raid over the City of London, causing twenty-nine fires in a very densely populated part of the capital. Twenty-two motor pumps of the London Fire Brigade were used to quell the flames and one fireman was killed.

As aircraft developed and their pilots' ability to pinpoint and successfully drop bombs on a chosen target improved, there came three major daylight raids by German aircraft over London during the summer of 1917. In one of these raids 162 people were killed, and many large fires were started despite the fact that most of the bombs had not been of an incendiary type. The government of the day seemed quite satisfied to accept the vulnerability of the capital to these air-raids and left the London Fire Brigade to cope with the ensuing fires with a fire-fighting establishment seriously weakened by conscription. There was, however, a later move to place outer London and industrial fire brigades at the disposal of the London Fire Brigade chief officer.

But the total tonnage of bombs dropped, together with the

fires caused by enemy action in the 1914–18 war, was relatively minimal. The Second World War saw the intense development of the *Blitzkrieg* as a strategic weapon of warfare, with the bombing by night and day of targets in the London area, the armament factories of cities and towns, and of many ports.

The capital itself bore the brunt of the early raids; from September 1940, the Luftwaffe came to bomb London on fifty-seven consecutive nights with as many as 300 aircraft in each raid. Wave upon wave of Dorniers and Junkers first dropped hundreds of incendiaries over targets, leaving the following aircraft to unload tons of high explosives upon the already blazing buildings far below. Many of the raids lasted for hours on end. Factories, docks, warehouses, offices, department stores, corner shops and rows of terraced houses all suffered the same fire and blast devastation. The battlefield had come to men, women and children in the streets of London.

During the early years of the war, the burden of fire-fighting in the capital fell on the professional firemen of the London Fire Brigade, together with about 23,000 auxiliaries called up at the outbreak of hostilities. In 1938 there had been a nation-wide call for volunteers to form a back-up force of firemen in case major air-raids took place. The men who rallied to this call in London came from many varied professions and back-grounds that included solicitors, journalists, artists, salesmen, drivers and labourers. Not a few were conscientious objectors.

Along with the men of the small borough brigades on the fringes of London, this collective army of fire-fighters faced the worst that the bombers of the Luftwaffe might bring. Yet most of the auxiliaries were quite uninitiated in the harsh and dramatic activity of tackling peacetime fires, let alone the conflagrations that broke out almost nightly as a result of the blitz raids. Nevertheless, from September 1940 the fire-fighters pitted their courage against whole areas of raging fire covering entire streets. Such fires were frequently termed 'officially out of control'. Hampered by shattered water mains, still-falling bombs, flying red-hot shrapnel, collapsing build-ings, together with a fireman's personal hazards of intense heat, blinding choking smoke, and swirling firebrands, the mixture of regulars and volunteers fought to prevent London burning. Such nights could be of the wildest sort and few other than wardens and police would be on hand to witness the firemen's battles.

Each morning, as the civilian population emerged from their home shelters or from the safety of the underground station platforms, they would see smoke and steam hanging low over the streets, drifting in the breeze through the windowless shells of the various buildings hit or burnt out during the night's raid. But most of the fires would be under control. As the firemen staggered around rolling up the cobweb-like mass of hose after their nightly struggle with the flames, most were weary, dehydrated, scorched, and covered in smoke stains, ash and dust. Many suffered from conjunctivitis, numerous cuts to face and hands, and body sores from the continuous chafing of ill-fitting uniforms that were perpetually wet through.

Yet it is strange to relate that these nightly heroes were the same men who, during the lengthy lull before the 1940 blitz, had been openly derided by some sections of the public as 'war-dodgers, loafers, parasites, and a waste of taxpayers' money'.

Following the last heavy blitz of 1941, there came another quiet period during which the government nationalised all UK fire brigades into one unified service. Many small units were able to benefit from a standardisation of equipment and training methods and improved communications in prepara-tion for a holocaust far worse than had been expected at any time.

The next stage of aerial warfare over London and the South East came in the form of the VI flying bomb, which at least gave some warning of approach before plummeting to earth. Then followed the horrific rocket-powered V2 that carried almost one ton of explosive. The London region once again bore the brunt of these weapons which brought a whole new dimension of problems for firemen and other rescue services. The problem of extrication of people trapped under tons of brickwork and rubble was compounded as the remaining upstanding structures creaked and swayed unsteadily upon their shaken foundations, often around the very scene of rescue. Gas from damaged pipes was another hazard which contributed to a number of fires caused by flying bomb and rocket incidents.

Throughout the war years, the women's section of the London Fire Service had contributed enormously to the overall success of fire-fighting operations. The women had been recruited from 1938 onwards into what had previously been an exclusively male domain, yet once the blitz started they more than proved their worth. The ladies of the fire service, many little more than teenagers, became drivers for petrol carriers, hose lorries and staff cars, and riders for motor-cycle dispatch work. They crewed mobile canteen vans which took hot refreshments out to the exhausted firemen at the scenes of fires, often while raids were still in progress, and they manned much of the communications network.

Consequently, when peace was finally declared in 1945, the men and women of the fire service in the London area had been more prominent than most of the home-front organisations. This is borne out by the large number of firemen and women killed and seriously injured in the line of duty, and the considerable number of awards for bravery won by members of the service. These included one George Cross and thirty-eight George Medals.

All this action had taken place during times when the fire service in London faced overwhelming odds in attacking huge fires, conflagrations beyond peacetime imagination. Yet no organisation which has included both a professional and an amateur element has ever gone smoothly and the London Fire Service was no exception. Early friction was not helped by the bad living accommodation provided for auxiliaries at most improvised, emergency fire stations. Yet the stresses of the 1940 blitz rapidly forged a link that unified the fire-fighting manpower against a common enemy.

This book tells of the endeavour, achievement and bravery of personnel of the fire service in London during the last war— a war fought in the streets of the capital against a dramatic backcloth of rampant flame and widespread devastation as the Luftwaffe waged terrible vengeance from the skies overhead.

I
Prelude to War

It had not taken the intense incendiary bombing of Madrid in 1936 during the Spanish Civil War to make the British fire service alive to the major risk of fire attacks delivered by enemy aircraft upon a civilian population. Indeed, fire service conferences held to discuss and plan a strategy for such an aerial war were held at the Home Office as long ago as 1933.

As the Spanish conflict developed, and the German air fleet was able to develop and perfect its bombing techniques and skills—all horribly demonstrated at the defenceless town of Guernica in 1937 where 2,000 civilians were killed in air-raids—London firemen could have been excused for wondering just how the brigade would cope under air-raid conditions. No doubt they had read the accounts of how most of the Guernica casualties had occurred—amid the fire and smoke of conflagrations which followed the bombing.

London and its administrative county area of some 117 square miles and a population of over four million, was at this time protected from the ravages of fire by a wholly professional fire-fighting force of 2,300 officers and men manning sixty-two fire stations. The London Fire Brigade with its well-drilled, experienced and disciplined personnel was probably the finest fire brigade in the world.

In the wake of the Spanish Civil War air-raids, the concept of incendiary bomb raids over London was fearsome. The whole London area offered itself as a vast and vulnerable target—most firemen had at some time or other attended massive riverside warehouse fires—in warehouses with each floor packed high with highly combustible goods such as fats, oils,

Taxicab towing unit with trailer pump – the basic unit of the AFS during the early years of the war. Note rolled lengths of hose in luggage compartment and fare meter still in position (*London Fire Brigade*)

Fordson/Sulzer heavy pumping unit attached to a Bethnal Green, East London, sub-station. Note pump prominently mounted on rear, two hook ladders on top of main ladder with rescue line and crew compartment behind main cab (*LFB*)

Hose-laying lorry showing method of laying ready-flaked large-diameter hose on the move to provide water relay from distant sources (*LFB*)

Women members of the AFS undergoing basic fire-fighting hydrant drill at Lambeth Headquarters, 12 June 1940. Immediately behind the group on the branch is a London Fire Brigade wheeled escape-carrying pump. The drill is under the watchful eye of an LFB Station Officer (*LFB*)

paints and grain. Each such building rubbed shoulders with the next in the maze of narrow Dickensian streets that ran down the edge of London's river. Here fire easily leapt from one warehouse to another like a mischievous escaping child. Often, fires in these buildings taxed the resources of the brigade to the full. Then there were the London slum areas where thousands of families lived in cramped and confined conditions which were a fire-fighter's nightmare. The City of London, the financial and insurance world, with its densely packed buildings had always been a high-risk area for the brigade, and the prospect of incendiary attack on the palaces, cathedrals, museums and other public buildings of London was in itself horrific.

Few people underestimated the damage that could be caused by high-explosive bombing, especially to the heavily-populated areas of London. In a report given to *Air-Raid Precautions News* in 1938, Duncan Sandys, MP, stated of the high-explosive bombing of Barcelona:

> In one place I measured the frontage of buildings that had been totally demolished, and found that it was well over 200ft in length. That is equal to about a dozen or so average-sized London houses. As might be expected, the buildings actually struck and those on either side of them have been reduced to a heap of shattered rubble. But in addition to this, other houses over a wide radius have suffered serious damage. Sometimes several hundred yards away windows and doors were blown in, steel shutters crumpled up, balconies ripped off, and partition walls, ceilings, and floors knocked down by the terrific blast of the explosion.

BIRTH OF THE AFS

As the war clouds continued to gather over Europe, people from both scientific and political fields added their own particular words of wisdom as to how best the threat of aerial warfare could be countered. J. B. S. Haldane made it clear in his book *Air-Raid Precautions*, 1938, that the expansion of fire brigades was necessary. Comfortingly for firemen, Haldane stated that brigade personnel should not be expected to patrol the streets during actual air-raids!

In fact, the first positive pre-war governmental move to co-ordinate fire service readiness for war was in February 1937, when the Home Office required local authorities to submit air-raid precautions and fire-protection schemes for their respective areas. There existed at this time 1,600 independent UK fire brigades under either county council, district or parish control. These brigades ranged from such organisations as the London Fire Brigade with its full-time crews manning 106 pumping appliances, down to the solid-tyred ancient motor pump and a handful of part-timers that typified many a rural brigade at this time.

Two separate Acts of Parliament reinforced the urgency to prepare the fire service to meet the threat of war on the home front. The Air-Raid Precautions Act of 1937 took effect on 1 January 1938 and made provision for a central grant to finance improvements in local fire-fighting services. This grant was as much as 75 per cent of the cost of improvements, and included the cost of the recruitment and training of a volunteer force to be known as the Auxiliary Fire Service that would supplement the regular brigades.

Later in 1938 came the Fire Brigade Act which embodied many of the recommendations of a committee set up in 1935 under Lord Riverdale. This committee's brief was 'to review fire brigade services in England and Wales and to advise whether any steps are needed to improve organisation and co-operation for the purpose of meeting danger from fire'. The Riverdale inquiry led to a section of the Fire Brigade Act that for the first time placed a statutory requirement upon the various county councils and other smaller local authorities to maintain *efficient* fire brigades. This Act did not materially affect the London Fire Brigade, whose constitution under an act of 1865 was little altered by the new legislation.

In December 1937, the London County Council as the

local authority controlling the London area, established its own air-raid precautions committee. This was presided over by Herbert Morrison, MP, JP. By March the following year, this committee had approved proposals for the recruiting and training of 28,000 auxiliaries for the London brigade. This number alone would require some 360 additional fire stations. There were to be two basic types of auxiliary—those who would in event of war relinquish their normal occupations and become full-time fire-fighters, and those who would remain unpaid part-timers and give what time they could during raids.

Although the first volunteers for the Auxiliary Fire Service (AFS) in London enrolled in March 1938, the initial numbers were disappointingly low. On 24 June 1938, the chief officer of the London Fire Brigade, Commander (later Sir) Aylmer Firebrace, CBE, RN (Retired), took part in a twenty minute BBC broadcast with Mr Herbert Morrison, in which an urgent appeal was made for men and women recruits. Sir Aylmer recalled in his memoirs that the broadcast did not cause the expected multitudes to flock to fire stations to join the AFS—it needed the Munich crisis later in the year to produce that effect.

This radio appeal marked the start of a concerted advertising campaign for AFS recruits. Large wall posters appeared throughout London, proclaiming: 'Keep the home fires *from* burning', and sixty AFS vehicles carried their mobile message through central London and the suburbs, exhorting the public to rally to the cause. On the Thames, a London Fire Brigade speedboat flew a bright blue 'Join the AFS' pennant, being primarily aimed at boating enthusiasts who would be ideal to supplement the small river section of the brigade. In the skies over the capital, two aircraft trailed a recruitment slogan.

In addition to all this activity came various recruiting meetings, including gatherings of the staff of several large department stores such as Harrods and the John Lewis chain of shops. Even employees of the Stock Exchange heard an appeal for auxiliary fire-fighters. From the outset, all this recruitment work fell as an additional burden on Firebrace's regular fire officers and following these meetings they must have been disconcerted at the poor response during those early weeks of the campaign. Few men and women came forward to sign up, although many wanted to know how to cope with incendiary bombs in their own homes.

Auxiliaries were enrolled in various categories according to medical and physical suitability. These categories ranged from men in class B—general fire-fighting duties; through class B1, which was officially described as modified fire-fighting duty and meant work at ground level only; to men fit only to man emergency fireboats of the river service (class B2). Women auxiliaries were initially placed in two grades, being either suitable for driving duties or telephone and office work. Youths of between fourteen and eighteen years old were placed on messenger and patrol duties.

Despite the poor response to the auxiliary recruitment campaign, in April 1938 the Press were invited to Brigade Headquarters at Lambeth to photograph some of the new recruits. By this time, 117 London Fire Brigade firemen had been detached from fire-fighting duties and appointed AFS instructors. The training programme for the AFS firemen initially took sixty hours, followed by a passing-out examination in both the theoretical and practical knowledge of fire service equipment. Included in the basic practical training for the class B and B1 recruits, was a considerable amount of hose running, ladder work and pump operating. At first, training was centred on regular fire brigade stations which had accommodation, catering and drill facilities able to cope with the increased number of men. On 11 April, AFS training had begun at Kensington, Bishopsgate, New Cross, Southwark, Clapham, West Norwood, Brixton and Streatham fire stations. Most of the men were trained and passed out by mid-June and then posted to headquarters.

Training of the women auxiliaries did not commence until late June, but by that time the first squads of the women's branch of the AFS were in full swing, with instruction going on at Shoreditch, Clerkenwell, New Cross, Southwark and Clapham.

From their inception, both the men's and women's branches of the AFS had their own officer structure, with people from a suitable 'background' (usually the professional classes) being appointed officers by the chief officer of the London Fire Brigade under whose command the whole AFS organisation functioned. This was to give the chief officer and his staff great problems in the months ahead, for as the auxiliaries were gradually merged with the regular firemen there were incidents of indiscipline between the AFS officers and lower-ranking, but far more experienced and proven, junior officers of the regular brigade. The problem was made more complex by the necessary interaction, as the London Fire Brigade and AFS were working so closely together. The AFS had no history or precedent, unlike the Army with its Territorials, or the Police with the Special Constabulary.

As the AFS developed in the later months of 1938, more and more difficulties faced the senior officers of the brigade. Accommodation for the auxiliaries was a major dilemma. The broad concept of wartime organisation called for a group of six AFS sub-stations to be sited strategically in each regular brigade fire station area. Each sub-station was to house one or more fire-fighting appliances manned by AFS personnel, but under the overall command of a London Fire Brigade sub-officer. It had been planned that most of the sub-stations would be suitable empty buildings or ones which could be requisitioned; into these categories fell garages, filling stations and schools. The latter had ample room in playgrounds for drills and PT and usually already had enough lavatories and washing facilities to cope with the large numbers of men expected to be based there once the full emergency scheme became operative.

The arrival of the first fully trained women members of the AFS also caused problems, one of which was the deeply entrenched attitude of many regular London firemen. Most regulars thought that the service had gone too far—surely fire-fighting was a man's job? The obvious need for separate and suitable female accommodation put an additional strain on the whole organisation as AFS numbers slowly multiplied with the growing threat of war.

EQUIPMENT

Amid all this activity, the very first of the AFS sub-stations were commissioned in September 1938. Three were in the City of London—in Moreland Street, Bunhill Row and Gravel Lane; the remainder were sited in the vulnerable and extensive dock area—at Surrey, the south-west corner of the West India, and London docks.

All the regular LFB 'red' fire engines remained stationed at their fifty-nine parent fire stations. These machines included pump escapes and pumps, each having a pumping capacity of 1,000 gallons per minute and carrying 1,000ft of 2½in hose; various ladders ranging from a 50ft wheeled escape, to the smaller but more portable hook ladder used by firemen to climb from floor to floor up the external face of a building. Some machines also carried breathing apparatus. Other fire engines in the LFB regular front-line included strategically sited turntable ladders, able to extend to 100ft. Headquarters station at Lambeth housed an emergency tender which carried specialist metal and wood cutting equipment, emergency floodlights and extra breathing-apparatus sets. A hose lorry was also available to provide a water-relay in the event of a large fire. The 'red' fire engines were a variety of Dennis, Leyland, Merryweather and Albion appliances. At the AFS training centres the volunteers were being trained to use the numerous types of pumping appliances needed in the event of war. These included two types of self-contained fire engines, not unlike the pattern of the regular red machines. Most were based upon a Fordson or Leyland chassis with a Sulzer pump able to deliver 900gpm; a heavier Ford/Leyland unit had a maximum pumping capacity of 1,400gpm (enough output to supply six powerful jets of water). All the emergency fire engines were finished in battleship grey and shorn of the normal splendid brass and chromium adornments.

There were also four types of trailer pumps designed for towing behind suitable vehicles, such as a light van or family-size saloon. These trailer pumps had a pumping range of between 120gpm and 900gpm and were manufactured by several companies, including Coventry-Climax, Worthington-Simpson, Dennis & Scammel (all these were on two wheels with pumps powered by four-cylinder petrol engines). Some Sulzer and Tangye trailer pumps were mounted on four wheels with pumps driven by Ford V8 engines.

All emergency equipment was provided direct to the brigade by the Home Office. It was delivered in a steady stream from mid-1938 onwards and besides the pumping units and trailer pumps came a great quantity of other fire-fighting equipment and stores, including miles of 2½in diameter hose. Most of the hose was American in origin and came in 50ft lengths, unlike the LFB's 75ft hose. An immediate problem with the imported hose was its couplings—it utilised a push-in-type instantaneous coupling; all the LFB hose had screw-type couplings. (Every fireman, both LFB and AFS, carried a hose-spanner as part of his personal fire kit.) The incompatibility of these couplings necessitated the issue of suitable adaptors for all pumps to allow hose lengths to be interchanged.

In addition, special 'radial branches' were issued. These were static nozzle-holders which could project a powerful jet into a fire, thus relieving firemen from the tough physical battle of controlling a reactive and snaking hose jet. Although such devices were already being carried by the LFB the radials were infrequently brought out by the regular firemen when a fire situation had been acknowledged as 'lost' and the need for vast quantities of cooling water over a long period was paramount. The issue of such equipment to the AFS was perhaps in anticipation of battles yet to come.

An interesting fact about trailer pumps is that they came with no towing vehicles—the brigade and AFS were expected to find what transport they could for this purpose. Although the LCC had already purchased sixty Fordson towing vehicles in order that the auxiliaries might perform drills with the trailer pumps, a number of Fordson light vans were also commissioned for the purpose of women's driving instruction. However, it was the London taxicab which proved to be the short-term answer to the trailer-pump problem. In September 1938, the taxicab committee of the Transport and General Workers Union wrote to Herbert Morrison, suggesting that a taxi might well be the ideal towing vehicle for fire service use, and such was the case. Strongly constructed, with a small turning circle and well able to carry a fair amount of hose, a short ladder and other fire-fighting equipment, over 2,000 were 'hired' by the London Fire Service before the outbreak of war. In many cases an agreement was made to 'hire' taxi drivers as well.

The most powerful of the trailer pumps were the four-wheeled versions, able to carry the additional weight of a heavier output pump, which were towed behind 'escape vans'. These were regular fire brigade 'red' vehicles that in peace-time carried a 50ft wheeled escape, quantities of fire-fighting gear, but lacked an inbuilt pump. The escape vans had the engine-power to pull the four-wheel pumps and added greatly to the front-line fleet of appliances.

The provision of more turntable ladders was a subject of continuing debate between the chief officer of the brigade and the Home Office. Turntable ladders were normally used for fire-fighting and rescue work from high buildings, being able to reach to 100ft (normally about seven floors). The London Fire Brigade peacetime establishment of these machines totalled sixteen and the chief, Commander Fire-brace, thought that in view of the city's fire risk in war, *every* LFB parent station should have a turntable ladder available. An additional forty-one turntable ladders were therefore requested from the Home Office. Naturally, the cost of all expenditure connected with equipping the AFS for war fell mainly to the government, which perhaps explains why the additional turntable ladders, the most complex and costly of all fire appliances, were slow in appearing.

Despite that problem, the arrival of other equipment provided by the government quickened as 1938 drew to a close, and storage space for vehicles and trailer pumps became a real difficulty. To accommodate 550 trailer pumps which could not be allocated immediately, a large store in Olaf Street, Shepherd's Bush was acquired until they could be sent to sub-stations as they were gradually commissioned.

THE AFS PARADES

During this time, the regular brigade continued to be ad-ministered with six districts, the river service having three fireboat stations along the Thames. LFB crews at stations worked a two-shift system in a working week of seventy-two hours, although supervisory and senior officers were on a continuous tour of duty and apart from their desk hours were liable to be called out to fires at any time! The LFB was the busiest fire brigade in the UK and its peacetime record showed that in the run-up to war it was kept extremely busy answering calls.

Alongside all the intense activity on the equipment and training front, was an equally frantic amount of installing telephone links between all the new sub-stations and their parent stations. In peacetime the LFB was either mobilised by exchange telephone or by street fire-alarms—the latter being connected to a fire-station watchroom. Although at this stage a final communications system for mobilising the fire service under wartime conditions had, surprisingly, yet to be agreed, a plan existed which did envisage the use of local control rooms under the overall supervision of a regional centre. Much of the training in the women's branch of the AFS was directed towards all aspects of communication and mobilisation of fire appliances. It was clear that in the event of war, this was one highly important area of fire brigade operations which would rely almost entirely upon the services of the WAFS.

Adding to the problems of the AFS, was a protracted difficulty about the issue of uniform. Although the Home Office had laid in a large stock of fire-fighting uniforms which included tunics, heavy serge trousers, waterproof leggings and boots, the brigade had only been allocated enough to supply each AFS man with *one* complete fire uniform. For some years, the regular LFB crews had been issued with spare tunics, trousers and boots, which allowed them, when they returned to their stations wet through and grimy, to change into dry clothes and have a fresh uniform ready for the next call. The situation for the AFS crews was less than satisfactory and, in spite of great and constant pressure on the Home Office by LFB senior officers, saw no prompt improvement.

However, putting a brave face on the problems, and as if to show their growing readiness for war, an AFS contingent took part in the annual Lord Mayor's Show in November 1938, the first time that AFS crews had paraded a large selection of their pumps and equipment in public. A further demonstration of AFS strength took place on 5 March 1939, when a long procession of its heavy pumping units, trailer pumps and other vehicles, threaded the streets of central London before their crews assembled outside County Hall to listen to an address by Herbert Morrison.

It is clear that the Home Office recognised the considerable experience of the LFB senior officers in planning the overall wartime UK fire service strategy. On 16 February 1939, the chief officer of the brigade, Commander Firebrace, and four

of his staff officers were seconded to the Home Office, for a
nominal period of three months, to draft a regional fire-
brigade defence scheme. In late March they resumed LFB
duties, having laid down broad guidelines for the regionalisation and grouping of many smaller fire brigades in the event
of war. Government spending on the AFS continued and in
April the Lord Privy Seal announced in the House of Commons that local authorities must accelerate Civil Defence
measures during the next three months even at the expense of
peacetime activities. The London AFS, of course, was only
one of five Civil Defence services being prepared for war.
The others—wardens, ambulances, rescue and demolition,
and repair work—were all being co-ordinated at a regional
level.

Further demonstrations of fire-defence readiness were
organised, including the annual review in Hyde Park on
3 June 1939 of both the LFB and the London AFS by their
royal highnesses the Duke and Duchess of Kent. This was
the annual event when the previous year's commendations
for bravery and long service medals were presented, followed
by a spectacular display of the brigade's expertise with all its
variety of fire-fighting equipment. The review took place
against a green backcloth of trees at the height of their summer
glory, in front of many hundreds of spectators. The royal
visitors, accompanied by Commander Firebrace, first drove
in an open limousine around the outer ring of the assembled
lines of men and women. Then the demonstrations began.
Several mock-up wooden buildings had been constructed
in the arena and here, in succession, pumps were set in motion,
ladders of all types were pitched against the buildings, and
the whole panoply of fire-brigade operations unfolded in the
various sequences. Many firemen also took part as 'casualties'
—dressed in nightshirts they cried out for rescue from upper
windows as their colleagues sprang into action with escape
ladders. Such was the enthusiasm of the personnel taking
part in this lifelike drama that several actually dropped their

own young children into the jumping sheets of firemen stretched out 50ft below!

The final item on the programme was entrusted entirely to the AFS and consisted of setting one of the mock buildings on fire. Once lit, the fire was allowed to grow to quite spectacular proportions until, at a given signal, thirty-two light vans swept into the arena each drawing a trailer pump, stirring up a great cloud of dust like some ancient charge of chariots. The heat from the blazing structure had begun to make the front-row spectators uneasy in their seats, but the crews soon had their pumps roaring into life, with hose run out and a crystal cascade of powerful jets of water directed against the inferno, which quickly died down under such a massive assault. As the ensuing black cloud of smoke rose into the bright sky over Hyde Park, momentarily casting a shadow over the assembly, few people watching could have failed to be impressed by the overall air of efficiency displayed.

WAR FOOTING AT LAST

In private, the service still recognised its own deficiencies: a chronic shortage of uniforms and accommodation for the AFS, and occasional non-acceptance of the system of AFS officer appointments. The inexperience of the AFS crews was also a worrying factor.

However, the brigade progressed more rapidly as the situation in Europe deteriorated, reaching something of a climax in the latter weeks of August. By this time detailed instructions on the mobilisation of sub-stations and their AFS fire engines were laid down. 25 August 1939 was the last day for 'passing-out' AFS recruits after their sixty hours of basic training. Five days later, steel helmets and respirators were issued to both LFB and AFS personnel and sandbag filling and protection commenced at all London fire stations. As if a postscript to all this activity, the Home Office finally announced the agreed weekly rates of pay for full-time auxiliaries. These were: £3 for men, £2 for women, 25s for youths aged 17–18, 20s for youths aged 16–17.

Although the brigade had already recruited a number of youths under sixteen for messenger work, the Lord Privy Seal announced that the government thought it undesirable to employ boys of that age on ARP work. Apart from that, many people in the LFB thought that the inordinate delay in announcing the pay rates had contributed to the poor recruiting response earlier. After all, asking men and women to commit themselves to a wartime obligation involving leaving their peacetime jobs was bad enough; not to be able to tell them the going rate of pay for their war fire-fighting duties was absurd.

During the last week of peace, the once overcrowded space of the vast Olaf Street warehouse was empty. Every one of the trailer pumps was now at a strategic point, over 570 being sent to London fire stations. Several hundred had also gone to reinforce brigades and their AFS outside the London area.

LFB reservists (recently retired full-time firemen and officers) received advance warning to stand-by in readiness to resume duties back in the brigade in their old rank, according to skill, experience and present ability. Some of them had been retired for several years and were aged fifty-five and over.

The GPO were asked to install telephone lines as a matter of priority to 103 schools now being used as sub-stations (these still did not have telephone exchange facilities) and on 26 August the GPO reported that all central London sub-stations had telephone lines completed and that eighty per cent of the outstanding communication work would be finished within ten days.

All LFB and AFS exercises were abruptly cancelled until further notice. Special hose and hydrant adaptors were distributed to all stations to enable LFB engines to connect to non-standard outlets on water supplies which might be encountered outside the London area at many factories and installations. Towing-bar attachments to allow the taxicabs to pull the trailer pumps started to be delivered to sub-stations, but until these could be fitted the trailer pumps were lashed to the taxi bumper as safely as possible, but there were many cases of the towing eye of the pump punching a hole in the back panel of the cab.

On 1 September 1939, the day that Hitler's troops invaded Poland, the final moves took place to put the London Fire Service on an established war footing. LFB personnel were recalled from leave and instructed to remain on duty at their stations. Earmarked vehicles and river vessels were placed in commission at action stations and many premises were quickly requisitioned. At 5.20pm, a telegram arrived at Lambeth Headquarters from the Home Office which cryptically stated: 'Emergency Fire Brigade measures. Call out AFS and proceed as in Home Office Circular 23/3/39.' Immediate steps were taken to bring the 23,000 part-timers into full readiness in the front-line fire defence of the capital.

Thus, as Neville Chamberlain broadcast to the nation at 11.15am on 3 September 1939, announcing a state of war with Germany, the LFS braced itself for the onslaught of fire from the skies. Dramatically, just as Chamberlain finished speaking, the first air-raid warning sounded over London. The adrenalin of all firemen and firewomen must have surged, but the 'raid' was not to be—after thirty minutes came the 'all clear'. This first warning was a result of a French aircraft arriving at Croydon aerodrome and some jittery but well-intentioned observers. 'At least,' remarked one AFS fireman at Lambeth as his crew stood down, 'the system works!'

The wailing of those first sirens marked the beginning of the London Fire Service at war; it was to be a long and at times arduous struggle against great odds.

2

Lull before the Storm

As part of the prearranged Home Office plan for home defence, the onset of war saw the implementation of a fire brigade regional scheme for the Greater London area and the outer suburbs. This was the direct result of Commander Firebrace's secondment to the Home Office along with a small party of LFB headquarters' officers earlier that year.

The London brigade remained a separate unit under the scheme and retained its peacetime organisation with defined districts, each being a group of fire stations and their respective areas. The LFB was, after all, the largest single brigade in the Greater London region, and covering as it did the very heart of the metropolis it made sound sense to preserve its identity and well-established lines of communication.

Firebrace, as the principal architect of the regional scheme, had planned that he himself would be the overall head of the region's fire-fighting resources, including retention of the command of his beloved London Fire Brigade. He had joined the LFB direct as an officer in 1919 after a successful naval career and progressed through the most senior ranks to become chief officer in 1938. But Firebrace's plans for his previous command were not to be. Unknown to him, his own regionalisation scheme had already been amended by Sir John Anderson, the Home Secretary, with the result that on 1 September 1939, Firebrace was required to relinquish his command of the LFB to take up a new post as London Regional Fire Officer. He wasted no time in appealing directly to the Home Secretary, and at a hastily convened meeting pleaded his case. The minister stood firm. Firebrace's deputy, Major Frank Jackson, immediately took over the command of the LFB and its Auxiliary Fire Service.

Besides the LFB, there were no less than sixty-six smaller fire brigades in the Greater London region, many of them only having one motor pump and a small territory to protect. These units were grouped into five districts, and placed under the control of the chief officer of the Ealing, Tottenham, West Ham, Beckenham and Croydon Brigades. These officers were designated Assistant Regional Fire Officers (ARFO). Each retained his own local headquarters and had a responsibility primarily for the co-ordination of fire-fighting services and their mobilisation in time of enemy air attack within their own districts. Part of Firebrace's regional scheme allowed each chief officer of the sixty-one remaining brigades autonomy to control his own men at a 'peacetime'-type fire, but in the event of a major fire in his area caused by air-raids, a chief officer could call for a small number of additional pumps from neighbouring brigades. If the size of the blaze demanded even more men and machines, these had to be sanctioned by the ARFO from his own district. If, in turn, the ARFO was unable to accede to the request for reinforcements, the scheme in theory required the Regional Fire Officer (Firebrace) to mobilise pumps from any part of the region, including the front-line red appliances of the LFB.

MOBILISATION

Once war was declared, AFS mobilisation moved very rapidly. By midday, Sunday, 3 September 1939, there were besides the 120 red engines of the LFB, almost 2,000 AFS motorised and trailer pumps, their crews based at over 300 sub-stations scattered across the London area. The last of these pumps had been equipped by scraping together every available piece of fire-fighting equipment.

All personnel, both regulars and AFS, were placed on a continuous duty system, day and night. This also included

Front line appliances of a typical London AFS sub-station, 37Y in Bath Street, Shoreditch, East London, June 1940. The vehicles are (from left): Heavy unit, towing unit with trailer pump, heavy unit, towing unit, and (far right) an officer's staff car. Note the spartan accommodation (*Frank Reader*)

The return to its native Thames of the fireboat *Massey Shaw* after its part in the Dunkirk evacuation. Several of the crew brandish rifles – note the three knotted climbing lines still trailing in the water. 3 June 1940 (*LFB*)

Hose-laying lorry blown by bomb on to roof of terraced house, Bonar Road, Peckham, South London. 7 September 1940. No trace of its driver was ever found and it was three days before the vehicle was located buried in the debris over one hundred feet from where the bomb had fallen (*Daily Mirror*)

administrative and workshop staff. At the sub-stations, the
AFS crews included men from many walks of life, some from
the professions, many from industry and not a few from
working-class backgrounds. Almost every man and woman
had reported to their posts in working clothes but even now,
forty-eight hours after call-up, there was evidence of confusion and a lack of clear organisation. Many AFS personnel,
although advised to report on 1 September with two days'
rations, brought none; indeed many had not had time to
prepare these when the telephones, telegrams and dispatch
riders brought the news of AFS mobilisation. Although the
sub-stations had telephones installed, many had no cooking
or heating facilities and personnel had to utilise what cafés
were available nearby. At many such stations, the early days
meant primitive sleeping arrangements on bare boards, and
often putting up with quite insanitary arrangements. Auxiliary Fireman Vic Flint kept a diary throughout his service
and recalls his early days at a sub-station in Whitechapel,
East London:

> No bombs—no fires! Which after all is pretty surprising to say
> the least. The siren yesterday (3 September 1939, soon after
> the declaration) put the fear of God into us. I must say I've
> never been so frightened in all my life—except, of course,
> during Munich week. This is a miserable place and I've already
> caught two lice. One managed to get in a couple of bites before
> I killed it. This is a London County Council Infants School, so
> I think the fire brigade must have brought the lice in along with
> the taxis and trailer pumps and telephones.

The state of some premises made available for the AFS
was appalling and few buildings were easily suited to their
new purpose. Auxiliary Fireman 'Mac' Young was posted to
Winsland Street sub-station in Paddington. This was sup-
posed to be located in a Great Western Railway recreation
hall, near the railway delivery stables. On 1 September 1939
this building was not ready for occupation by Young and his
twenty-four AFS colleagues. They were forced to spend their

37

first night as full-time firemen bedded down amid the straw along with 200 restless GWR horses and about 10,000 flies. There was no food and no washing facilities. Although they were able to move up to the empty top floor of the stables the next day, it was some days before the sub-station proper was commissioned and two taxis with trailer pumps delivered. Even then, Young and the others were forced to scrounge some timber locally to construct some primitive bunks.

Some AFS personnel were lucky in being attached to the LFB fire stations where living conditions were of a higher standard. Auxiliary Firewoman Peggy Joseph reported on that first day of September to West Hampstead Fire Station and was immediately given the job of driving a staff car. She recalls that one of her first impressions was the LFB station officer's rage when another AFS girl reported after dark and pulled the brass handle on the station frontage. This action caused every call bell throughout the station to ring and brought the duty LFB crew sliding down the poles within seconds of the alarm, only to find that it had been raised by an embarrassed female.

A different experience befell Auxiliary Firewoman Owtram. She had turned up after the call-up at her sub-station which was located in a public garage with a large loft above:

We had been told to bring blankets and a supply of food. But one or two girls had brought neither. Of some fifteen women, only three wore uniform. The rest had joined the service within the last two days. We gathered in the mews, amiably smiling and, as regards most of us, utterly lost. It was useless to climb the ladder; the loft door was locked. The men had not yet arrived. By the wall of the garage was heaped a small pile of sandbags. They were symbolic only. They could be used to no purpose in the loft. The rain fell lightly. The darkness gathered. 'This simply can't be true,' said, I suppose, the inner voice of each one of us, while we exchanged cigarettes and feeble jokes.

The men arrived. They were forceful and efficient. The company officer ran up the ladder, smashed with his axe the broken balustrade of a gallery, unlocked the door, called us all to come up and, a little after, called the roll in the garage below.

Yet in spite of the extreme hardship of some sub-stations and the different social backgrounds of the AFS crews, there quickly grew a common bond against the enemy threat. This helped to ease the early rigours of sub-station life, and the fear of what would be the outcome of the raids which were expected at any time. Auxiliary Fireman Frank Reader joined the AFS at Shoreditch exactly a year before the outbreak of war. He remembers the first hours of 3 September vividly, when the first air-raid sounded.

It had been clearly spelt out to his group, during training lectures by the LFB instructors, that the incendiary-carrying capacity of the Luftwaffe aircraft was immense. Frank Reader could think of nothing but those racks and racks of incendiary bombs when his sub-station quickly went on alert during that first day of war.

Another immediate effect of war was a change in the way that AFS recruits were trained. Before the outbreak of war, all recruits were enrolled at their nearest fire station and usually undertook their sixty hours' basic training there. One of Firebrace's last orders as commanding officer of the LFB on 3 September 1939 was to stop this arrangement. A procedure was introduced whereby all recruits were enrolled at six district training schools around the London area. One indication of the rush-recruiting measures in operation was that an AFS recruit no longer had to undergo a medical examination; he was merely asked to sign a declaration that he was physically fit and capable of undertaking duties of a strenuous nature!

ANTICLIMAX

During the first week of war, the AFS did some heavy work, mostly filling thousands of sandbags, not only for fire stations, but hospitals, ambulance stations and supply depots. However, after a week had passed, it gradually became clear that there was not going to be the threatened lightning strike by the Luftwaffe. Also obvious was the fact that the existing 2,000 AFS pumps and crews could not be maintained at this level of readiness on a permanent basis. Shifts were re-introduced and leave again allowed to all personnel on the forty-eight hours on duty, twenty-four off, pattern. Accordingly, following the agreement of the Home Office, the first-line strength of the AFS pumps was reduced to 1,500. First-line pumps were those manned and ready at *all* times. Part of the wartime scheme had been to station a trailer pump and crew near each street fire-alarm in a well-sandbagged position, but with 1,700 such alarms in the LFB area, the reduction in the number of front-line pumps meant the progressive withdrawal of crews at these points. This, not unnaturally, aggravated local business people and many private individuals, who had felt reassured by the visible presence of a uniformed fire-brigade unit close by, ready to deal at once with any occurrence. Despite these protests, concentrating all AFS resources at sub-stations meant that a much-needed opportunity to sort out the hurriedly assembled equipment was now available. Leave, sleeping and messing could be re-arranged on a much more organised basis.

The lack of raids by the Luftwaffe during those early weeks of war was seen as a godsend by all those concerned with AFS training, billeting and equipment. But at no stage was the threat of fire bombing far away—a brigade war memo issued to officers in charge of stations was headed rather sombrely:

> AFS officers are to realise that they may at any time have to take command of a sub-station, and at fires, and they must be ready to do so. If disasters occur in London the responsibilities which may fall upon AFS officers may be very great.

Recruiting to the AFS had reached such a pitch by the end of September, that Major Jackson was forced temporarily to stop accepting fresh applicants; 2,700 men and women recruits were enrolled at the new district training schools during the three weeks following the declaration of war, and the whole recruiting and training system was in severe danger of collapse.

Major developments were taking place in the provision of additional water supplies for fire-fighting. The LFB hierarchy had recognised that any high-explosive bombing would soon render parts of the existing underground networks of water mains useless. Most of these mains were of cast-iron piping which was very brittle; most of them were only a few feet underground, and were unable to withstand heavy explosions without fracturing. The majority of street fire-fighting hydrants were fed from these mains.

Such was the cost of the large-scale improvement of London's water supplies that, back in July 1938, the Home Office and the Treasury had agreed a government grant to the London County Council of some £500,000 for this sole purpose. As a result of this, work was in hand to lay additional 24in steel mains to carry water purely for fire-fighting use. The extra mains ran: from Dowgate Dock, near Cannon Street railway station, right through the City to the Grand Union Canal (Regent's Canal) at City Road; from the Regent's Canal through Regent's Park, down to Oxford Street and on to a point just north of the northernmost point of Shaftesbury Avenue; from Charing Cross to Trafalgar Square; from London Docks to the City Road.

In view of the extreme fire risk of the City area bounded by Cheapside, Aldersgate, Chiswell Street and Moorgate, short spur mains to augment existing supplies were planned. This area included St Paul's Cathedral. Work was also commencing on the fitting of 200 fire hydrants on large-capacity trunk water mains that would not normally have them. Most street hydrants fitted to public mains gave water at anything between 25 to 50lb per square inch, although this figure depended upon how many other pumps were drawing upon the same main. The hydrant pressure would normally be boosted by fire service pumps to produce up to 150psi at the nozzle—this would give a powerful jet of water with a long-reaching throw.

To ease the water-supply problem, the Home Office had made available to the LFB a considerable quantity of 6in diameter steel piping. This came in short lengths and was usually laid in the edge of the road against the kerb. Its drawback was that it required several four-man crews to work together to connect up the pipeline as it was unloaded from lorries. Brigade officers considered that laying such a pipeline was a very slow process and preferred to use a hose lorry—these were able to dispense about a mile of ready-stowed 3½in rubber-lined hose continuously at about ten miles per hour. Plans were in hand at the outbreak of war to commission forty hose lorries to supplement those the LFB already had.

Another major water resource was the 1,000 gallon portable dam which was introduced to all London units in the autumn of 1939. These were carried rolled-up by the AFS sub-station units, yet could be quickly erected to provide an open-topped water tank. The original portable dams were of canvas construction and when full of water measured approximately 12 by 10 by 3ft high. During early 1940, they were supplemented by static steel-panelled 5,000 gallon versions: these were installed and kept full of water at many strategic sites on street corners and were clearly marked 'Emergency Water Supply'. The dams, intended primarily as a first-aid fire-fighting measure, because most fire pumps could empty 5,000 gallons in a matter of minutes, were expected to be of the greatest value to crews if used as a reservoir supplied by a hose relay from a distant source. By keeping a dam thus full, it should be possible to operate several pumps from it independently of any other sources.

But the search for fire-fighting water went beyond this—LFB officers surveyed the contents of swimming baths, large tanks on private premises and lakes, ponds and even paddling pools in London parks. A plan existed to lay surface, light-weight pipelines from the Serpentine in Hyde Park and the Round Pound in Kensington Gardens to strategic points on the edges of the parks. There were, of course, the River Thames and Dockland, but because of tidal ebbs and flows, the extraction of large quantities of water was clearly a job for fireboats, some of which were capable of lifting as much as 4 tons of water a minute from the river, passing this vast quantity through their own hose lines to the most convenient on-shore point for further distribution. The fireboats each had a fixed deck-mounted monitor-nozzle for projecting a powerful water jet onto any riverside fire. Accordingly, as the AFS had grown during the approach of war, so too had its involvement in the river section of the brigade. In peacetime, the LFB had a fireboat operating from each of the three floating fire stations on the banks of the Thames, at Lambeth, Black-friars and Cherry Garden Pier (Bermondsey).

Under the Air-Raid Precautions programme, the Home Office had provided ten fireboats for the AFS, each being equipped with fire pumps of similar capacity to the three existing LFB craft. By January 1940, in addition to the three LFB river stations, the AFS were crewing the ten extra fireboats at six river section sub-stations. Eight dumb-barges were also acquired, to act as platforms from which pumps could be got to work, being towed into position by tugs.

THE 'PHONEY WAR'

As the days and months of waiting grew, there was an ever-increasing strain upon London's auxiliaries whose morale began to sag. In almost every sub-station, the AFS were herded and crammed together, some in deplorable accommodation, mostly without adequate means of recreation or even a wire-less with which to while away the night hours. Many sub-stations still lacked proper washing facilities and several stations in the Dockland area were downright insanitary. Although mattresses had been issued to AFS personnel at sub-stations, there was still a critical shortage of blankets, despite a nationwide BBC appeal several weeks after war was declared.

In a move to alleviate the growing boredom that was being generated by the almost daily repetitive AFS training exercises in Dockland and at strategic City sites, in early 1940 Major Jackson gave permission for certain AFS crews to attend fires alongside the LFB men, which previously they had been barred from doing. The outcome was hardly surprising. In the early hours of 24 January 1940, in sub-zero temperatures, the brigade was called to a large warehouse of seven floors in Oval Road, Camden Town. The fire had got a strong hold and developed into a thirty-pump affair requiring the attendance of 466 officers and men, of which over 300 were auxiliaries, as yet quite inexperienced! The fire was not under control until almost 11am that morning, and by then 3 officers and 9 firemen were injured. Of these, 2 officers and 3 firemen were AFS personnel. The total number of appliances used included 29 LFB pumps, 6 AFS pumps and 37 AFS trailer pumps. Major Jackson later commented: 'It was demonstrated that at difficult fires of this nature, a stiffening of these comparatively inexperienced personnel by regular firemen is most essential if the efficiency of the fire-fighting organisation of London is not to be impaired!'

As the weeks of 1940 passed and still no air-raids came, public feeling towards the AFS changed and they were viewed in a less favourable light. Many exercises were held to test AFS readiness, covering a considerable distance around London and using as many as a hundred pumps each time; it seemed that the public liked to see the AFS busy at every conceivable moment. Before long, various nicknames emerged— 'the Darts Brigade', 'Duckers', 'Parasites', 'Idlers' and '£3 per week Army Dodgers', being the most common. However, even if some AFS recruits were intent on avoiding conscription, they must have had little comfort in their present 'safe' environment as London firemen; on 3 January 1940, it was confirmed that the AFS was not a reserved occupation, and that those of them between twenty and twenty-five could in fact be called up—there were rumours in the ranks that the upper limit was soon to be extended to thirty years.

The overall effect of this loss of trained men to the armed services produced a serious manpower shortage. Added to this, the regular LFB strength had been gradually depleted since September 1939, because reservists were being conscripted. This was partially offset by the selection of physically suitable AFS men for an intense three-week training course, using regular brigade equipment, after which they were posted to regular LFB stations as 'Red Riders', working alongside professional firemen of pre-war years. For this privilege, the selected AFS men were paid an extra five shillings a week.

Frank Reader was one of these selected men who were able to enjoy the better messing and sleeping accommodation of a regular LFB station. As a Red Rider, he was posted to Shoreditch Fire Station in October 1939 for a spell of two months. Here he rode as a crew member on one of the two LFB appliances stationed there. He still recalls a distinct feeling that the professionals had a 'holier than thou' attitude towards the AFS interloper, and this was no doubt exacerbated by Reader's AFS tunic badge and grey steel helmet. Nevertheless, he was at least able to attend a number of peacetime fires in the Shoreditch and Hoxton areas of London and get a first-hand look at the smoke, sweat and grime of real firefighting.

But even outside the service, AFS morale and its standing in the public eye continued to fall. Many men left, including some of those who had rallied to the early call back in 1938—solely because they were disgusted by the treatment now being afforded them and preferred to volunteer for the forces or other war work rather than to be eventually conscripted.

Another AFS grievance was the introduction of the Civil

(Personal) Injuries Act common to all ARP services. Under this act an AFS man or woman who was sick or injured was discharged from the service after two weeks of incapacity. Worse could follow: the victims of this harsh act frequently had to suffer the indignity of a means test in order to qualify for help from the Unemployment Assistance Board.

Michael Wassey was another AFS man who kept a diary during this frustrating period of waiting for the Luftwaffe. As a trained fire-fighter himself, he was probably better armed than most to comment on the scene. In March 1940 he wrote:

> What is it that has caused the enthusiasm and patriotic fervour of the AFS in the early days of mobilisation, to degenerate in some cases into what almost constitutes surly acquiescence or, at the best, indifference to their job in the fire-soldiers' front line?
> ... The national fire-fighting scheme as a whole is efficient, and there is no question as to the fire-fighting abilities of the AFS Section. Nor have the AFS any quarrel with their professional brothers and leaders. When intensive air-raids begin, the percentage of casualties expected to occur among the personnel of the AFS is amazingly high—far higher than those expected in any other section of ARP.
> We know the risks we take, and we accept them. They are not the reason for the ever-growing numbers of resignations weekly that are causing concern in Parliament, at the Home Office and on local councils.
> What are these reasons?
> Perhaps the most important is the contempt displayed by the endeavour to treat AFS members, not as civilian volunteers, but as workmen in uniform. The spirit of the early days is forgotten, when men were induced to come into the AFS at £3 a week for the duration (though £3 is less than the majority received in civil life), and when promotion was freely offered to the keen and willing. Latterly the volunteer has found himself more and more subject to open 'discipline', although the essence of discipline was already there. Any officer who knows his job gets discipline without enforcing it, and any man accepts his reasonable orders without debate.
> The AFS was deeply hurt, alas, by unkind innuendoes in the

national press. The newspapers, on the whole, were being far from understanding. We appealed to their sense of fair play. . . .

It is the firm conviction of every AFS man that the press has failed to give the AFS a square deal.

Newspaper men with practical experience of the Spanish war, Poland and Finland, can be relied upon always to regard us as the front line of Home Defence and in every sense as soldiers. No cheap heroics are wanted, but reporters are reminded that news must be based on fact, not opinion, and that in time of war it is more than ever necessary to acknowledge the work of the AFS. Some of these lads may live to thank us for digging them out.

For the older men of the press, we have the healthy respect they have for us. They know what has been done elsewhere and what we shall be called upon to do.

We ask them for a square deal. Knowing them as we do (there are many of us in the AFS who come from Fleet Street) we know we shall get it. Good-natured chaff we like. Cheap jeers from the unimaginative are resented.

By April, requests for resignation from the AFS were rife and brigade officers were powerless to stop the exodus of hard won and trained men and women. The numbers were so worrying to the government that they hurried through a statutory order which forbade full-time members of the fire service from resigning. Had this order not been made, London's fire defence would have been a shambles. As it was, almost 50 per cent of AFS personnel had left by the time the order took effect in June 1940.

The Red Riders, the regular firemen of the old LFB, had also made their first war sacrifice. Under a pre-war negotiated agreement with the Fire Brigades' Union, the regulars had been promised a shorter working week of sixty hours from 1 January 1940. They were now working, on average, 110 hours a week on duty. Added to these depressing conditions was the very cold winter of 1940. Anti-freeze for vehicles based at sub-stations was scarce. Many heavy and trailer pump units and taxis stood out in the open and had to be started up and run every quarter of an hour throughout the night. Even the street water dams froze solid.

Against the background of a harsh winter and an obviously unhappy relationship between some regular firemen and AFS personnel, a committee of inquiry sat and heard evidence from many interested parties. After much deliberation, the inquiry recommended a broad scheme of unification and proposed that every officer position be filled by either LFB or AFS personnel on promotion. This scheme was initially introduced in September 1940. Under it, promoted AFS men were given relatively equal status with the regulars regarding pay, uniform and service conditions, thus causing more disquiet among some regular firemen who objected to being officered by 'amateurs'. Equally unsurprisingly, some AFS men thought that too many of the new officer positions went to regulars.

FIREMEN IN FINLAND

However, the still-distant rumblings of war came a little closer to the London Fire Service in March 1940 following the involvement of Finland in the war. AFS volunteers were needed to provide a basic fire-fighting unit. Over 600 men came forward virtually overnight, although the aim was to send only a small unit of nine fire-fighters with a heavy pump unit, a hose lorry, 3,000ft of lined hose, breathing apparatus and a host of small equipment.

The selected nine flew out to Stockholm whilst the vehicles and equipment followed by sea. By the time the London fire-fighters arrived in Sweden on their way to Finland, peace between the Russians and Finns had been declared. The party became caught up in the evacuation of areas ceded to the Russians, and being isolated by the German invasion of Norway, ended up as 'full-time' members of the Helsinki Fire Brigade. During ensuing months, the AFS men attended many incidents, large and small, and were able to bring their fire-fighting expertise to bear with great effect. Unfortunately the Finns still relied upon German goodwill for their trade to pass through the Baltic to the outside world and consequently, when the Germans requested that the Finnish Government stand down the British contingent, they had no option but to agree. The London firemen (some of whom were ex-teachers), found ready employment as English teachers and two ended up as university lecturers. When Germany attacked Russia in June 1941 the London unit proceeded to a Swedish internment camp and returned home via Portugal.

STILL WAITING . . .

Back in the London region, and into the spring of 1940, firemen continued to wait for aerial bombardment. Morale was still low and public feeling remained hostile about the apparent inactivity of the AFS element of the service. Indeed, AFS men themselves coined a new phrase, *Sitzkrieg!* Amongst complaints received at this time at brigade HQ at Lambeth, was one alleging that AFS crews with their taxicab towing unit had been seen at a wedding. Subsequent investigation proved that all personnel involved were off duty and that the petrol used was supplied by the owner of the taxicab—his daughter was being married.

Individual discrimination against firemen was also rife; it seemed that in public houses throughout London, auxiliary firemen in uniform were always the last to be served . . .

3

Baptism by Fire

During the spring of 1940, the severe anticlimax resulting from general lack of war action and the low morale prevailing in the LFS, was suddenly and unexpectedly boosted by the first two LFS involvements in enemy action. After the massive build up of fire-fighting units ashore they, surprisingly, saw the river section in operation. Although this section of the brigade had a number of fire-fighting vessels in readiness, including three custom-built LFB fireboats, most of the fleet was hastily commissioned during the approach of war. They were shallow draft vessels equipped as floating fire engines. For months they had lain prepared for the expected air-raids over London and like their land-based colleagues the fireboat crews had experienced many, many exercises and hours of drills, yet no real action, apart from the occasional 'normal' occurrence of fire in the immediate vicinity of the Thames and Dockland.

On the evening of 11 May 1940 a Dutch boat, the SS *Prins Wilhelm Van Orange*, was attacked by enemy aircraft off Flushing. A single incendiary bomb penetrated the ship's hold and a deep-seated cargo fire soon threatened the entire vessel. She put into the Thames Estuary and six LFB fireboats, including the *Massey Shaw* (the LFB's newest regular fireboat), were sent to deal with the smoking *Prins Wilhelm Van Orange* at a point off Gravesend. Unfortunately, the fire had burned for some hours and despite the efforts of the fireboat crews the Dutch vessel sustained severe damage.

DUNKIRK

Following this first direct skirmish in war, it was the *Massey Shaw* and her crew that were again in action a few weeks later. On Sunday 26 May, the evacuation of the British Expeditionary Force from the beaches of Dunkirk had begun. By the following Wednesday, the operation was in full swing, with some 38,000 troops lifted out of danger on that day alone, many on to small craft able to get close enough inshore to the queues of men awaiting evacuation. Large oil tanks at Dunkirk were set on fire by enemy bombing and the troops on the beaches were under constant aerial attack.

With the eyes of the nation on the drama on the French beaches, on Thursday, 30 May, the Admiralty asked the brigade for the use of the *Massey Shaw* as part of the small-boat armada which was going to the rescue of the BEF. At this stage it was anticipated that the *Massey Shaw*'s specialist capacity would be used to provide a fire-fighting unit amid the throng of rescue craft.

The *Massey Shaw* was at this time stationed at Blackfriars Bridge, being named after the brigade's famous Victorian chief officer, and had been completed at Cowes in 1935. She was 78ft long, with a beam of 13½ft, and yet was only 3ft 9in in draught. The boat had a registered tonnage of 50, with twin screws each of which was driven by a 160 horsepower diesel; at a fire, these diesels were disengaged and the engines powered the fire pumps. Her top speed in calm water was 12 knots.

Over the preceding days, whilst the *Massey Shaw* rode the tide at her moorings in the shadow of St Paul's, the crew had paused in their brass polishing to watch many tugs as they passed down river towing strings of lifeboats, skiffs and dinghies. By Thursday the men had heard rumours that *Massey Shaw* was going to Dunkirk; later that day volunteers were called for. A crew was hastily selected from a positive flood of fireboat crews who wanted to give their services across the Channel, and consisted of a station officer, two sub-officers and four regular LFB firemen of the river service plus six auxiliary firemen. This was a larger than normal fireboat crew, but it was anticipated that they would spend some days fire-fighting off the French coast. All four LFB firemen were qualified coxswains and one had been an RN signalman. Surprisingly, none of the AFS personnel had so far had any instruction in operating the engines and fire pumps and were taken purely as working hands.

There followed a very hectic and intensive afternoon at Blackfriars pontoon as gear and stores were collected and stowed. Soon after the selected crew arrived and took over, the *Massey Shaw* cast off and headed down river for the open sea. Other than her initial delivery from the Isle of Wight shipyard, *Massey Shaw* had never been to sea; indeed with her low freeboard she had not been designed for anything other than river work and she was a difficult craft to handle, even on the Thames. One of the first tasks as the fireboat proceeded past Greenwich and the Royal Naval College was to commence painting over all the gleaming brasswork with a service grey.

Being unable to navigate safely once darkness had fallen, the *Massey Shaw* moored overnight at Holehaven until first light on the Friday morning. The crew were under orders to call at Southend Pier to confirm that they were to proceed to the French coast; the hourly situation at Dunkirk was changing rapidly and no one really believed that the evacuation could go on much longer. However, the message at Southend Pier was clear—proceed to Ramsgate Harbour. A chilly easterly wind was blowing up under an overcast sky and on the beaches of Dunkirk this was beginning to produce a surf which was making boat-boarding an extremely hazardous operation.

The *Massey Shaw* arrived off Ramsgate Harbour about 1pm on Friday, amid a crowd of small vessels of all sorts, bobbing at anchor. *Massey Shaw* was the only representative of her type. Within two hours, as soon as the LFS crew were joined by a RN sub-lieutenant armed with a chart and steel helmet, the London fireboat was under way for Dunkirk. On board, they soon learnt that they were *not* now going as a fire-fighting vessel, but as an additional craft to ferry troops back home. As *Massey Shaw* cleared Ramsgate, homeward-bound ships, laden down with troops, ponderously made their way to safety.

The chart provided set out a clear course through the minefields of the Channel. Although the smoke pall over Dunkirk was clearly visible within an hour of leaving Ramsgate, *Massey Shaw* was handicapped in that she had carried no compass prior to this trip and in the haste to fit one before departure from London, no magnetic adjustment had been made. Consequently, the compass was little more than a rough guide and despite the boat's shallow draught there were frequent tense moments as she crossed areas of swirling water clouded with sand as the Dunkirk beaches loomed nearer. Floating wreckage was all around and every ship heading towards home had more khaki on deck than seemed possible.

Once anchored as close in as possible off Bray Dunes beach late that Friday afternoon, the crew of the *Massey Shaw* lost no time. Against a continuous background cacophony of the explosions of falling bombs, machine-gun and rifle fire, to-gether with an intermittent anti-aircraft barrage, two firemen dropped into the light skiff normally towed by the fireboat and pulled through the surf to the nearest line of soldiers stretching out into the water.

Unfortunately, after an initial reluctance to negotiate a few feet of surf towards the skiff, about eight soldiers quite suddenly made for the small boat and despite protests from the two firemen, attempted to climb aboard. The skiff tipped and quickly sank in about 4 feet of water. The soldiers, including several non-swimmers, and both firemen made for a small motor-boat nearby, from which all were transferred on board the *Massey Shaw*. The LFB station officer then conferred with the RN officer, as it appeared impossible to commandeer another skiff or small dinghy—all were in use, ferrying men between the waiting ships and shore.

Then followed an abortive attempt to put a line on to a small RAF launch which was aground in the shallows and drag it to the *Massey Shaw* along with a load of troops. After two unsuccessful efforts to secure a rocket line to the launch, the RN officer, together with a fireman, swam ashore with the line and together they made it fast to the launch. As *Massey Shaw*'s capstan took the strain, about fifty soldiers awaiting rescue jumped up onto the launch which, once clear of the sandbank, became hopelessly top-heavy. *Massey Shaw*'s crew protested and swore at the troops to no avail—they stayed put on the swaying launch. In the swell of the tide, the towing line came adrift and the launch, with the soldiers still aboard, drifted helplessly back towards the beach.

Darkness was now falling and with an ebbing tide the water was becoming dangerous. The RN officer was still marooned on the beach and for some time the crew of the *Massey Shaw* manoeuvred the fireboat up and down amid the wreckage of sunken lorries and small boats in an attempt to locate a small dinghy or suchlike. A boat was eventually found but communications with the shore proved difficult. Another fireman swam through the breakers with a line and the boat was then rowed to a queue of soldiers waiting in the water. Once more the efforts of the firemen were thwarted when the line to pull the boat back to the *Massey Shaw* came undone.

By 11pm, the RN officer had returned to the fireboat via another small rowing boat he had found, and despite the strong tide and darkness another attempt was made to bring more troops on board. Two of the fireboat's crew rowed back to the beach, tied a line to a nearby partially sunken lorry and began to ferry a queue of Royal Engineers back to *Massey Shaw* using the line to guide their passage across the swirling water. Before long, the fireboat had taken so many soldiers on board that she was beginning to ship water over her deck and the crew ceased the ferrying activity, swung *Massey Shaw* about and set off for Ramsgate. It was still pitch-dark—and the craft was still without a reliable compass. On the way back across the Channel, the *Massey Shaw* had a near miss when an enemy aircraft several times attempted to bomb her. Although the bombs missed, the spray they caused drenched the men on the overloaded boat.

When Ramsgate was reached at about 7am on Saturday morning, sixty-five soldiers were disembarked. Some had been so closely packed into the forepeak that there was difficulty in getting them out. All were wet through and most had been seasick.

After a quick breakfast, the *Massey Shaw* was refuelled, cleaned up below decks and soon on her way back to Dunkirk. Sub-Officer May, who had been at the wheel on the first trip, and two auxiliary firemen volunteered to return and the Naval authorities this time put a small group on board to act specifically as a beach party for loading the troops. They also took a 30ft ship's lifeboat in tow.

Having returned to the beaches around 11pm on Saturday, the crew found more partially sunken wreckage and obstacles, and with a falling tide navigation was hazardous. But the growing fires from around the town gave enough light to work by and thankfully the clouds of smoke drifting across the beaches made air attack less likely. Perhaps amid the drifting smoke the London firemen felt a little more at home. As the process of ferrying soldiers from the shore to the *Massey Shaw* began, so too did an artillery attack on that section of the beach and many shells burst close around the fireboat. When about 100 men had been loaded on board, *Massey Shaw* moved out to a troopship standing further off at anchor in deep water and, despite a considerable swell, transferred the soaked and exhausted troops.

Whilst heading back towards the beach for a second load, the port main diesel engine failed and it took half an hour to restart; during this time *Massey Shaw* was very hard to manoeuvre between the assorted wreckage all around. Then, as more soldiers were being taken on, stretcher cases began to arrive, which were not easy to get aboard the fireboat and subsequently up onto the troopship. During these early hours of Sunday, *Massey Shaw* ferried over 500 men to the troopship before she too, now heavily overloaded, lifted anchor, intending to head for home.

Massey Shaw returned to her sector of beach to pick up her own landing party and whilst in the shallows many soldiers clambered aboard, almost grounding the fireboat in the swirling tide. When they finally left that part of the beach, they were the last vessel to do so, at about 3.30am on Sunday morning, disembarking forty troops at Ramsgate about four-and-a-half hours later.

With a fresh fire service crew sent from London, the *Massey Shaw* again left for Dunkirk that evening. This time the fireboat was initially taken alongside a high jetty full of troops, but in the darkness the steep drop down into her was too difficult and *Massey Shaw* was forced to leave empty. In the confusion, an auxiliary fireman who had scaled the slippery structure in an attempt to make the fireboat fast, was left behind. He eventually found another ship and returned home safely.

After yet another brief stop-over at Ramsgate the next morning, *Massey Shaw* was ordered back to London as the great operation of evacuating Dunkirk was almost over. But more drama was in store for the fireboat. Off Margate, *Massey Shaw* was slowly overhauled by a French ship, an auxiliary naval vessel *Emile de Champ* which, when about 200 yards abeam, suddenly struck a mine and sank almost at once. The *Massey Shaw* was able to pick up about thirty men from the water, all badly injured, and take them back to Ramsgate.

Early the following morning, *Massey Shaw* set off again for her Thames mooring and as she came up river, the fire service crews of previous trips were taken out to her by motor-boat and she thus came up to the fireboat station at brigade HQ at Lambeth with her full crew of 'Dunkirk' firemen. Naturally, the *Massey Shaw* was enthusiastically cheered as she passed each river fire station; the wives and mothers of all on board were taken to the landing stage at Lambeth to greet her, where she was also met by the commanding officer of the LFS, Major Jackson.

As the fireboat tied up and rang off engines, fire service history had been made. Over 700 troops had been rescued by the *Massey Shaw* during the three trips to Dunkirk. Most surprisingly, the boat was unscathed by gunfire or shrapnel, her crews uninjured, although the vessel did suffer minor collision damage, like most other small craft, as she was thrown against larger ships during the hectic ferrying and transfer operations.

Sub-Officer A. J. May, *Massey Shaw*'s coxswain, was awarded the DSM for his services. This was a rare naval award for a non-serviceman. Auxiliary Firemen H. A. Wray and E. G. Wright were mentioned in dispatches. Vice-Admiral Sir Bertram Ramsey, KGB, flag officer commanding Dover, wrote in the *London Gazette*:

> Of the civilian manned craft one of the best performances was that of the London Fire Brigade fire boat, *Massey Shaw*. All the volunteer crew were members of the London Fire Brigade or Auxiliary Fire Service, and they succeeded in doing three round trips to the beaches in their well-found craft.

BUILD-UP TO THE BLITZ

However, the LFS euphoria over the fireboat's epic trip to Dunkirk soon dispersed into the malaise which existed before that historic week of the war. Exercise after exercise, endless spit and polish and the poor accommodation at sub-stations continued. Even the occasional opportunity for AFS crews to supplement the Red Riders at ordinary fires came few and far between. The pre-war LFB regulars were generally able to cope with most major outbreaks; hence even when a sub-station attended a peacetime fire in turn, there was little firemanship to be learnt at a single small incident. With 360 sub-station crews all clamouring to go to fires, it was not an easy task for officers of the LFS to keep sagging morale from falling to an all-time low. The sub-stations and their personnel were each born out of the build-up to war, yet still no real war came to the fire-fighters of the London region.

But as each week passed, a variety of events in the brigade continued to set a scene that showed the fire service's operational readiness for war, yet reflected the 'life as normal' theme of London's population—a population as yet untouched and unharmed by the war. Many pumps now carried protective suits in anticipation of gas attacks, but a relaxation of 'night attire' orders in May 1940 indicated that senior officers were, wherever possible, trying to make life more bearable for the thousands of waiting fire-fighters.

LFB *General Order 310 8 May, 1940 :*
Dress for immediate duty at night—With the exception of riders of red appliances, despatch riders detailed to follow red appliances, the crew of the 'duty' machine at each sub-station and night duty men on river craft, personnel of. LFB and AFS need not sleep in their clothes between 10pm and 6.45am.

Until this order, *all* personnel on night shift had had to remain fully dressed, ready to go. Whatever lay ahead for the men and women of the LFS, it was clear that some fire service scenes would be graphically caught for posterity—facilities were granted to any professional artists now enrolled in the AFS to sketch or paint during leisure hours *or* when on duty, provided that the 'proper discharge of duties is not interfered with'.

During the first week of May 1940 the brigade's 'War Diary', which was maintained at headquarters, briefly recorded that at Lord's an LFB cricket team beat an eleven from the City Police. No details of the innings were mentioned; no doubt it was the result that mattered.

THEN THE BOMBS CAME

Then, in the same week that the LFB team took to the hallowed turf at Lord's, the Luftwaffe began to make sorties across the Channel and over parts of Kent. Bombs fell near Canterbury on 9 May, and suddenly the months of waiting appeared to be nearing an end. Single air-raid warnings, given to the London area by sirens, were becoming more regular from June onwards, particularly in the early hours of the morning. Each initial 'yellow' warning (preliminary intimation of air attack) put all LFS crews at 'stand-to', ready to turn out to any outbreak of fire as rapidly as possible.

On 8 June, high-explosive bombs fell in open country at Addington in Surrey and again, three weeks later, in fields at London Colney, Herts. Michael Wassey wrote:

STAND BY YOUR PUMPS!
The testing hour is here. At no time has the prestige of the AFS stood higher than it does at this solemn moment. Let there be no amazement at the situation. We have been expecting it and the AFS has not been paid for nearly ten months without the full knowledge that we are here for a purpose. Forget the derision, the off-handed treatment by certain persons, now so swiftly cured of their fixed ideas. There is but one purpose, one endeavour, with which we must occupy ourselves—to give as we have never before given in our lives and play our appointed part in the defence of our country.

Let us face facts. Courage, initiative and contempt for danger will be as typical of the AFS throughout the country as it was of the redoubtable *Massey Shaw*, the Thames fire-float that helped in the magnificently organised evacuation of the BEF. But let no man confuse bravery with recklessness. Brutally put, it must be understood that in our work one live fireman is worth all the dead ones, and one fit fireman worth ten thousand wounded. We speak frankly because it is the solemn duty of every fireman to take no undue risks, and above all to keep calm and to keep his head.

Sir John Anderson appeals for more AFS men. On the radio Mr. Norman Birkett, KC, said the nation would live to thank the 'men and women who have for months now stood so nobly and patiently by their posts'. Alas, what numbers would have still remained but for the folly that led the Ministry of Labour to conscript them for the services already too swollen to need them.

During mid-August, with the first week of the Battle of Britain under way, sporadic lightning raids by the Luftwaffe on RAF airfields nearest to London at Biggin Hill, Croydon, Kenley and Hornchurch, took place. A Croydon fire officer recalled:

At that time I was residing near the airport. It was a warm summer day . . . No barrage balloons were flying. Suddenly the loud drone of aircraft engines was heard, but I took no particular notice of this, for aircraft were constantly flying over Croydon. Soon they came into sight, flying in perfect formation . . .

I watched the escorting fighters leave the formation and the bombers carry out a line-ahead manoeuvre. No sirens had been sounded, and I was still under the impression that they were our own planes. Then I saw the German markings very clearly, and immediately ran indoors to telephone the fire service and police. As I was speaking I heard the explosion of the first bomb, and part of the ceiling of my dining-room collapsed . . . There was an auxiliary fire station near the airport, and crews were actually running out hose on the aerodrome whilst the bombers were making their run on the target. The raiders completed their task without interruption.

Under the London regional scheme, the LFB sent a number of pumps to assist the Croydon Brigade in dealing with the aftermath of this raid. German bombers also singled out the large fuel-tank depots at Thameshaven, about twelve miles down river on the Essex shore of the Thames. Yet it seemed clear that the Luftwaffe had still not marked the capital as a target area.

It was not until the night of 17 August that the first recorded incendiary bombs fell on the London area. They occurred at Woolwich and Eltham, both in the south-east suburbs, and caused nine minor fires that were quickly dealt with by local fire-fighting units. Michael Wassey was prompted to write:

On the eve of the new decisive phase of this bitter war and to every man, woman and boy in our service—stand by your pumps, God be with you and let your courage, determination and bravery merit your acknowledged place at the head of the Civil Defence Services.

It must have surely looked to most firemen serving in the London area that the long months of waiting were almost over. In fact, air-raid warnings through late August were quite commonplace—seven separate alerts were sounded on 18 August alone.

On the night of 24 August came another German raid on the large fuel-tank depot at Thameshaven. This was to be a fateful night of the war on the home front and for the LFS. Two enemy aircraft, seeking the Thameshaven target amid the incessant anti-aircraft fire, apparently failed to locate the riverside tanks and their flammable contents. The Luftwaffe crews, conscious that they dare not return to France with their bomb loads intact, found the flak becoming increasingly heavy. Having flown well past their correct target area, the bombs were dropped and the two aircraft turned for home.

Underneath the incoming path of the German planes lay the City of London and the East End, and as they approached, the air-raid sirens sounded at 11.08pm. This was the sixth alert of the day. As the pubs were dimming their lights and emptying of people and the inhabitants of the City and East End settled down for the night, the misplaced bombs came whistling down.

One of the first sticks of high explosives scored a direct hit on St Giles, Cripplegate. All along Fore Street on the northern fringe of the City square mile, incendiary bombs clattered onto rooftops, each bursting spontaneously into a small, glowing, intense ball of fire. On impact, some incendiaries penetrated unseen through roofs into attics. Others lodged in guttering high up over the street, like incandescent candles. The first LFS units from Redcross Street and its satellite sub-stations were on the scene within a couple of minutes, but a serious fire situation had developed. Flames were already burning through the roofs of several premises and many others were threatened as thick, black, rolling clouds of smoke spiralled high into the night sky.

The second of the off-course German aircraft had discharged its bomb-load further east over the dock area and a similar fire situation to that at Fore Street was rapidly developing in the West India Docks. Apart from the death and destruction caused by high-explosive bombing, incendiaries had set fire to the roofs of two separate dockside warehouses. Local fire stations were soon emptied of regular and AFS crews and a quick reconnaissance by the first firemen at the scene intimated a huge fire threat to all the surrounding buildings.

By mid-morning the next day and after hours of intense fire-fighting the fires had been beaten, although crews were to remain at the scene cooling down well into the evening. The raid provided a clear illustration of the sheer number of pumps and manpower required in time of air-raids. At Fore Street 200 pumps were used—mainly AFS heavy and trailer pumps, backed up by a number of LFB appliances. Each pumping unit carried a four to six man crew. Most of the AFS crews at this fire had never seen a fire such as raged all along Fore Street that morning. Indeed, many LFB regulars, with years of experience in peacetime London fire-fighting, had rarely seen such fire devastation. In fact, before the war, a thirty-pump fire was considered a major outbreak. And Fore Street was the result of an isolated bombing by a *single* enemy aircraft.

At the two major fires in the West India Docks, one required 100 pumps and 2 fireboats; the other 70 pumps and 6 fireboats. Elsewhere in East London, the LFS attended two other major blazes—one a thirty-pump job and the other requiring twenty appliances. During the early morning of 25 August, the brigade was also called to forty-eight minor fires. Many of these were caused by burning brands flying from the major fires, lodging on roofs and window-ledges of unaffected properties downwind.

The following morning, and in the harsh light of dawn, the charred blackened ruins steamed as crews damped down what remained. The wartime fire-fighting system had been tested and all the outbreaks in the City and docks had been contained and eventually controlled. Hundreds of AFS crews had been blooded, and although no fire-fighter had been killed, many had been injured during the sweat and toil of the night. The normal hazards to a fireman—falling slates, tiles and brickwork and shower upon shower of burning fragments—had taken their toll.

Air-raid sirens sounded many times during the next few days and nights and during the first week of September 1940, but no further direct bombing of London took place. However, in late August the London Fire Region sent 117 pumps, 5 water and 3 foam units to various major fires outside London, providing fire cover for south-eastern districts where home appliances were detained for many hours at fires caused by air-raids; in this way thirty London firemen went to Dover to relieve local personnel. The river section was in action yet again on 4 September, when bombing caused a large fire at Tilbury Docks and in two ships moored on the Thames. Several London fireboats spent twenty-four hours on station at these incidents, and at one *Emergency Fireboat no 5* was involved in a collision with another craft during fire-fighting operations and sank. All fire-brigade members on board were rescued.

THE THAMESHAVEN RAID

The fires at Tilbury were the result of Luftwaffe persistence in attacking targets along the Thames Estuary and effective raiding continued to take place, aimed at the large fuel depots at Thameshaven, Shellhaven and Purfleet. At Thameshaven, a heavy high-explosive raid on the morning of 5 September set five of the large 2,000-ton oil tanks alight. The local fire brigade unit had little equipment or large enough numbers of men to deal with such a major situation. Petrol and oil fires demand a concentrated attack with foam to seal off the surface of the burning liquid from oxygen in the atmosphere; such a task requires tens of thousands of gallons of foam, carefully applied.

In the late afternoon, the LFB were asked to send fifty pumps to Thameshaven, but as the London reinforcements would be well outside their normal area the officer-in-charge of the LFB force was given clear instructions that, upon arrival, he should work under the control of the local officer. Several hours later, as the London crews and appliances approached from the west, a huge column of smoke marked their destination.

James Gordon, who before the war had been a journalist on *The Daily Telegraph*, joined the AFS the day before war was declared. He was one of the several hundred LFS firefighters who went to the blaze at Thameshaven on 5 September 1940. He wrote:

> ... Now they could see the surging line of appliances behind them. The big units were competing with each other for position, swinging out into the road like rogue elephants, passing and being passed. A scarlet appliance of the regular fire brigade passed them in a glitter of brass and new paint, zooming up the road at a steady seventy. An old engine of pre-1914 vintage chugged steadily and obstinately behind them although their speedometer flickered past sixty. They clambered out of the cabin and stood on the suctions, clinging to the ladders with one hand and making rude gestures and V signs with the other.

Then, well below the horizon they saw a great black banner of smoke which hung in the air like the menace of a pirate flag.

'That's our job!' shouted Ginger, leaning forward into the cold slip-stream of air so that his words were lost. The smoke rose higher and higher as they raced down the level road. They turned through the gates of the oil-plant and were in a new, desolate world.

It was low, marshy land broken by radiating concrete roads. Clusters of gigantic oil tanks were spawned against the skyline. The roads were torn by bomb craters, as though the land itself had protested and spewed ragged chunks of concrete. Out of some of the craters protruded iron stanchions to which were tied fluttering rags. These denoted the menace of time bombs.

They bumped slowly over the broken roads, quietened by the horror of destruction. The burning tanks flung up dense, black oily smoke which looked almost solid and effectively obscured all signs of flame. Past tanks battered, squashed and melted into fantastic shapes. Past men unrecognizable in squelching veils of oil. Oil oozed into the soil and over the roads like black blight.

The officer-in-charge, his brass epaulettes smeared and deadened, gave them their orders and directions in a voice made hoarse by bawling over the mêlée.

They were all dismayed, even Tommy and Ginger. Their tunics were new, their boots and leggings well blacked. Now they were ordered to get to work on a burning tank which stood in a concrete pit which was deep with oil.

They set the Heavy Unit to work under some scaffolding bridgework and unrolled their clean hose and saw it submerge into the oil. They procured a foam-generating tank and began to set it up in the oil pond. One by one they reluctantly jumped over the parapet and, wading knee-deep in warm oil, began to capture empty drums which floated on the viscid current. These they opened and held under the oil until they filled and sank. Then they piled one on top of the other until they made a slippery platform on which they set up their foam generator.

Hervey shouted timid orders from outside the pit until they indignantly demanded that he come in with them. He walked towards them gingerly, holding up his arms like a tight-rope walker. Suddenly he disappeared into the oil with a horrified glug. He had stepped into a bomb crater. They pulled him out and laughed, then went on with their work.

The order was sent back to Mac for water, and the long, awkward branch became alive as, pointing upwards like a gun, it delivered its ammunition of foam into the oil tank which boiled and belched like a volcano. The top was red-hot, and as the fire took hold lower and lower in the oil, the steel melted and drooped inwards into the seething fire. The sides were pierced with machine-gun holes and hot oil spurted into the pit in steady streams.

Paul, on the front of the branch, guided the thick jet, his mind recoiling on itself at the horror and nearness of danger. He kept wetting his lips with his tongue. Whenever he lowered his eyes he was confronted with the nightmarish landscape. It was unreal. It couldn't exist. Yet here he was inches from an awful death. His mind burrowed back frantically at the memory of quiet, sunlit streets and level lawns, but his body struggled with the weight of the branch and the heat and the smell of oil.

'Do you realize that if some of that burning oil falls into this pit we shall be fried?' he asked quietly.

'I s'pose so,' said Fred miserably. The bag of sweets in his pocket was saturated with oil, and his palate longed for the tartness of an acid drop. He was a mug to have volunteered for this job. If anything happened to him, his wife and kid would suffer. He felt the oil creeping up his leggings and wondered what his wife would say about his ruined pants.

The situation was desperate. The contents of five tanks were fiercely alight and seven other large tanks close by were threatened. In several of these, the oil contents were beginning to stir with the radiated heat and the metal plates of the tank sides were buckling. However, in the view of the local officer-in-charge, the situation could be contained without most of the LFB contingent and he asked all but five London appliances to return home. Alas, an hour later as darkness was falling, and with the tank fires roaring in the background, the local chief reported to the LFB senior officer that as he was a volunteer, it was time for him to go and see to his business matters! This left a few scattered local fire-fighters and the small LFB force hardly making an impression on the fires that clearly marked the site for any returning Luftwaffe bombers. To add to the firemen's problems, the air-raid sirens wailed out the first warning of the night.

As the crews stuck to their overwhelming task, the London officer telephoned his HQ and demanded his forty-five pumps back. He was told that he could not ask for this—the responsibility for that area of Essex was with the local rural district brigade's officer. However, Major Jackson, London's chief, no doubt realising what was happening, sent Lieutenant-Commander Fordham, a senior and greatly experienced LFB divisional officer, hurriedly to report on the situation. When Fordham arrived at the tank fire he quickly saw its seriousness and himself rang LFB HQ for more men and appliances. He too was told that it was not his responsibility to order additional pumps and that the regional commissioner for Number Four Region (Essex and East Anglia) was being contacted. This happened to be Sir William Spens, Master of Corpus Christi College, Cambridge.

After a further delay, during which two other oil tanks caught fire from radiated heat, it was learnt that a Cambridge region officer was on his way. Fordham, renowned throughout the LFB as a direct and aggressively forthright officer, could hardly have been pleased with the infuriating delay. After half an hour, a sports car bumped over the lines of hose and drew up near the blazing tanks. Its young driver informed Fordham that he was from the Cambridge Borough Surveyor's Department and had come to take charge. He told Fordham that he had never been to a fire before, although he had attended an ARP fire-fighting course of a week's duration. Fordham got the young man to telephone at once for fifty pumps and three fireboats, and told him to watch—the LFB were taking over. Soon the LFS pumps were arriving, guided eastwards by the huge flickering orange glow in the night sky.

By daybreak, the fire-fighting operation had been well organised and an effective foam attack had been launched onto the tanks from close range. Many crews, like James Gordon's, worked up to their necks in hot oil to get close enough with their foam jets. Occasional German aircraft bombed the site and strafed the hundreds of firemen with machine-gun and cannon fire, and it was only those crews taking a well-earned hot drink at the canteen vans who were able to take cover. The enemy strafing went on sporadically all day on 6 September. Frank Reader was one who drove the reinforcing water units that had been sent to Thameshaven the previous night. He had travelled to the Essex coast along with other appliances from his Daniel Street, Shoreditch, sub-station. Frank can remember a pre-raid remark by a Royal Artillery sergeant in charge of a nearby newly installed anti-aircraft-gun emplacement. 'Let them try again tonight,' he gloated. As the sun dipped low in the sky the Stukas droned high overhead, seemingly to pass uninterested over the smoke column marking the oil tanks. 'There you are,' called the sergeant, 'they're not interested in us now we've got this baby.'

But the Stukas were merely positioning for a direct attack out of the sun and their incendiary bullets were soon strafing all those around and thudding into the burning tanks. The noise of the anti-aircraft fire, the screaming Stukas and the appliances pumping at high revs created a cacophony of sound. As the fires came slowly under control, many of the LFS crews made up their gear and prepared to head for home. With aircraft overhead James Gordon recalled:

The superintendent stood silhouetted against the skyline, looking down at them.

'You boys can suit yourselves,' he said hoarsely. 'I don't blame you for taking a bit of shelter. But the sooner we get our stuff made up, the sooner we can get away. Otherwise we might be out here all night.'

They scrambled to their feet and out of the ditch, following him through the bright sunlight. He pointed to the lines of hose he wanted them to make up. Back in the oil-pits again, walking carefully for fear of bomb-craters. Plunging elbow deep into the oil for hose. Heaving it out hand over hand, inch by inch because of the slippery footing beneath them. The intolerable

The morning after a raid. Damping down operations in progress in Oxford Street, W1., with the burnt-out shell of John Lewis & Co., in the centre of picture. Note the dangerous high unsupported wall. 18 September 1940 (*LFB*)

The damage caused by high explosive bombing to underground water mains and other pipework is clearly illustrated in this view of Tottenham Court Road, W1., looking north. 24 September 1940 (*LFB*)

At the height of a raid, three firemen attempt to get a line of hose to work whilst the building burns out of control. Note upward direction of flames from first floor windows caused by the vast quantities of hot air being swept up, which in turn is firing the floor above. Fifty Shilling Tailors, Piccadilly, W1. 11 October 1940 (*LFB*)

A crew begin to retrieve their appliances following a raid on Endell Street, Covent Garden, W1., that has partially damaged the sub-station. 15 October 1940 (*Daily Mirror*)

oily stench. The slimy serpents of hose which sometimes ended in nothing. Burned through.

Out of the pits again, to wrestle with the obstinate hose which had become hardened and unpliant. They couldn't roll it up in the usual way, but had to make a two-handed job of it. One stood on the coupling while the other walked round him again and again as though winding a capstan. Round and round until they had rolled a huge wheel of hose. Length after length. Pile after pile littering the flat land. Couplings, branches and lines. An immense paraphernalia like that on a battlefield.

The engines of the appliances began to rev up, and the wheels began to roll slowly over the debris. Each vehicle was loaded to capacity with oil-oozing equipment and moved forward over the shattered roads. Out of the gates and onto the smooth arterial road where the treads gripped once more and the engines droned into full speed.

The way back was a triumph. The road threaded through towns and suburbs where people turned and saw the grey and red appliances with their loads of oily men and hose. They cheered them as they passed.

Ginger stood on the suctions and took the cheers as though he was a prince and waved his arm in royal salute. The others grinned at him and borrowed cigarettes from each other.

As they passed through Romford, the sirens howled a warning. Ginger took the cheers as though they belonged to him. What were sirens now?

On the afternoon of the next day, Saturday 7 September 1940, the Luftwaffe bombed Thameshaven again and set fire to the undamaged oil tanks. The LFS was once more asked to send immediate help and a number of pumps was dispatched.

But most were to be recalled to London before nightfall; as the Thameshaven bound appliances headed yet again down the Essex coast arterial road out of East London, across the Channel squadrons of German bombers were being loaded at their airfields with thousands of incendiary and tons of high-explosive bombs. For the very first time the Luftwaffe target was to be London; their clear directive from Marshal Hermann Goering a simple one—to raze the capital city to the ground. The London Blitz was about to begin.

4

Fire over London

Around 4pm on Saturday 7 September 1940, the first German aircraft swept across the Channel and were soon over the Thames Estuary. Some of the bombs again fell upon the flame and smoke scarred tanks of Thameshaven and started several oil fires once more. However, the bulk of the first formation of over a hundred Dorniers and Heinkels droned on westwards high above the line of the Thames, heading for London. The bombers had a fighter escort with them and once over the course of the river proper, anti-aircraft fire started to harass them. Hurricanes and Spitfires were soon engaged in dogfights and as they wheeled and turned the duelling aircraft traced patterns high in the clear afternoon sky. Yet the huge wave of bombers swept on until they were over the eastern edges of suburban London. The London air-raid sirens had sounded their preliminary warning at 4.33pm; the first German bombs, high explosive and incendiary, were whistling down on West and East Ham, the Royal group of docks, Canning Town, Silvertown and Woolwich Arsenal with its large ammunition dumps. Minutes later, further up the river, bombs rained down upon the vast complex of the Surrey Commercial Docks, whose quays and warehouses were high with one and a half million tons of imported timber.

In a matter of minutes, hundreds of terraced houses, shops and factories were struck. Many received direct hits and were blown apart. Fires quickly kindled and took hold. Right across this eastern end of London, and even as the second wave of enemy bombers closed in, the first of the fire calls were already coming in to fire stations. From East Ham, just outside the London County Council area, right into the eastern districts of the LFB area, fire crews were turning out.

With bombs still falling, the fire situations in both the Royal and Surrey Docks soon looked serious. The Royal group was in fact outside the London County Council area and was thus controlled by the Assistant Regional Fire Officer at West Ham. Such was the rapid and almost uncontrolled growth of fire within the Royal Docks that within half an hour of the raid starting, West Ham Control were asking London Regional Control at Lambeth for 500 pumps.

Although the first local appliances and crews on the scene had quickly got to work with several powerful jets of water, these hardly made an impression on the growing and roaring flames. Trying to get pump suctions down into the unlimited deep water of the dock whilst the concussion of high-explosive bombs shook the ground under their very feet was hardly something the firemen had practised. Yet despite the flashes and the explosions, the water came up to the pumps, and more hose lines were run out towards the fires.

The surrounding area of streets of terraced houses outside the docks were soon threatened and East Ham and Barking Brigades requested urgent assistance from the LFB. But Major Jackson, in charge of the LCC area, had by now his own problems to cope with. The first fires at Quebec Yard, Surrey Docks, at Rotherhithe, fed by successive showers of incendiary bombs, had quickly reached such proportions that after a brief reconnaissance by the local station, Jackson was forced to commit a further 200 pumps to the scene. Another 500 were divided between the north bank group of docks below Tower Bridge—London, St Katharine's and West India. At the latter, thousands of gallons of rum were already ablaze in one large warehouse and liquid fire poured out across the surface of the dock basin, providing an awesome sight for the crew of the first fireboat on the scene.

Peter Blackmore was an AFS fireman whose sub-station was among those first to respond to the dockland fires. He recalled:

One evening in September, when I was on guard duty, the usual wail of the siren sounded. I looked away towards the east and wondered what stray plane had trespassed into the London Defence Zone, causing so much noise on such a tranquil evening. A few over-anxious mothers, with their babies, bed-clothes and sandwiches, perambulated self-consciously past to take refuge in the now almost empty Tube shelter. According to rule, I put on my helmet and strapped my gas-mask to the alert position and stood near the appliance-room door, with one ear cocked for the telephone.

Away in the distance guns sounded and flashes could be seen on the horizon. This was not unusual, but what was strange was the ominous red glow in the sky, which, had it not been in the east, could have passed for an indifferent sunset. I was watching this when the relief patrol arrived. 'What's that over there, Harry?' I asked.

'They're here, mate. They're bombing the docks.'

'Good Lord!'

'We shall have a drop of work tonight. You'll see. Better go and have a drink while you've got the chance.'

I remembered with pleasure that I was on Joe's pump and that Paddy was on it too. Paddy, as his name implies, being an Irishman, full of much natural charm and friendliness.

In the watchroom the girls were agog with excitement. In fact every one seemed pleased that something had happened at last. I went into the canteen and had a drink, and just as I was about to drown it with another, down went the bells. Yes, we were to move eastwards, towards the sky which no longer resembled an indifferent sunset, but which leapt with light.

The streets seemed unreal and eerie, each one echoing a fire-bell moving towards dockland. Above, one could hear the purring of enemy planes and ahead the rushing sound of bombs falling. A great pall of smoke was rising, the barrage balloons shone crimson in the sky.

Joe always drives at full speed, and this night our unit would have qualified for Brooklands, until, as we drew near the target, we became part of an endless queue of appliances, all steadily moving up and being detailed to their exact positions. Bombs were falling fast and heavy now. We did a great deal of ducking, and I for one don't mind confessing that my heart was in my mouth. The journey towards a blitz, like most apprehension, can be the worst part of it.

At one point the traffic was suddenly stopped. Somewhere ahead a bomb had made a crater in the road, and we, only too ready for an excuse to take temporary shelter, cowered close to the wall of a high building, deriving great comfort from its apparent protection, until the mounting flames showed our protector to be an oil refinery annexed to gasworks. It sent us skedaddling back to the pump, and it was with relief that we greeted the starting of the traffic once more.

Eventually we came to a standstill at the wharf where we were to spend that endless night. Everything seemed to be on fire in every direction, even some barrage balloons in the sky were exploding. The cinder-laden smoke which drifted all around us made one think of the destruction of Pompeii.

THE THIN RED LINE

Up to 7 September 1940, four-fifths of the London auxiliaries had never seen a real fire, and yet here they were being called upon to deal with outbreaks that in peacetime would have taxed the skill and stamina of hundreds of experienced regular firemen, and this in the face of continued bombing all around.

But the thin red line held. By the time the 'all clear' mercifully sounded at 6pm, the intense raid had lasted non-stop for one-and-a-half hours. The results of the first concentrated bombing of London were plain for all to see. Looking eastwards down the Thames from Charing Cross, the evening sky over dockland flickered and glowed orange with the leaping flames. Occasionally, great spiralling clouds of smoke obscured the infernos, and the reflected light from the fires showed up many miles distant like the intermittent flashes of some gigantic thunderstorm.

As AFS motorcycle dispatch riders made haste from incident to incident through the smoke and rubble in the streets and reported back to local fire controls, the immensity of the firemen's task became clear. By 6.30pm the large wall map at Lambeth Regional Fire Headquarters, which normally displayed pegs to represent the availability and location of

London's hundreds of fire-fighting units, looked decidedly bare. Logged alongside this chart was the overall fire situation: this already showed nine conflagrations—a fire service term meaning a fire officially out of control and rapidly spreading—these included the huge fires at Surrey and London Docks. In addition the situation board showed nineteen thirty-pump and forty ten-pump fires, plus over 1,000 smaller incidents.

Reinforcements rushing to the Surrey Dock fire met heavy congestion, caused mainly by other fire appliances. The senior LFB officer at the scene had repeatedly asked for more and more appliances to be sent. In peacetime, the crews of extra pumps sent on to a large working job have a duty to report to a central control point first. Upon such fireground organisation depends the success of fire-fighting operations. However, with so many fires to assess that night, little real control or co-ordination in the early stages was possible.

A request went out at about 7pm for a further 100 pumps and as these converged on the main roads serving the dock area around Rotherhithe, there were traffic jams caused by heavy pumps and trailer units trying to get into the dock via the various gates. Some confusion reigned. There were no proper reporting points for those arriving and no single LFB officer was ready to meet and deploy the new arrivals to maximum advantage. The leading-firemen and sub-officers in charge of pumps in most cases just got their crews to work as best they could.

The whole position was further overshadowed by another air-raid warning which sounded around 8.30pm. Lambeth Regional Control was informed that this was another 'red' alert, meaning 'aircraft imminent'. Within minutes, more waves of aircraft swept across the London sky, but unlike those leading the first raid earlier in the day, the Heinkels and Dorniers of this first concentrated night raid did not need to search for their targets. They merely unloaded their deadly burdens upon the vast areas of fire several thousand feet below.

Firemen manning branches and pumps from Whitechapel to West Ham now found they had to stand their ground as the bombs began to fall again. Red-hot shrapnel bounced off buildings and clattered into the streets around the feet of fire-fighters as they tried to keep their powerfully hissing jets of water pouring into the raging flames. The concussion effect of the high explosives shook their spines.

Surrey Docks was a 250 acre nightmare with a fire zone already covering one whole square mile. Incendiaries had not only settled and started fires in the deck cargoes of many ships awaiting unloading, but had also fallen on to the upper-most part of the 20ft high stacks of tinder-dry softwood and various types of resinous timber stored throughout the open area of the dockside. Within half an hour of the first bombs, fires here had spread from timber stack to stack with the rapidity of a forest fire. Even the wood-block-paved roads were alight. Such was the heat given off that jets of water turned onto the burning stacks only momentarily extinguished the flames. As the firemen swayed their jets around to cover the maximum area of fire, they discovered that the doused stacks steamed, dried out, then burst forth into flames in less than a minute. Burning embers, some a foot long, from Surrey Docks were sucked up into the tremendous updraught of scorching hot air and floated off to settle on some nearby roof or ledge to start yet another outbreak. One of several fireboats which ran the gauntlet of the lee bank of the Thames opposite the Surrey Docks entrance, in order to get downriver, soon had its paintwork blistered from end to end. The dockside cranes slowly weakened and sagged under the intense heat; one by one they leaned to one side, then keeled further over and finally crashed, sending a shower of sparks up to join the ascending mass of fiery fragments soaring into the night sky.

Four nearby auxiliary sub-stations within the dock area itself had to be abandoned and soon all were totally engulfed in the flames. With over 500 pumps and their crews at work, the local LFB regular fire station, Pageants Wharf, became the focal point of operations; here, several times, AFS fire-women had to leave their control positions and communications duties to tackle numerous small fires that threatened the building. These women also ran a forward dressing station for the many fire-fighters brought in suffering from burns, cuts and hot embers or fragments in eyes, or those simply blinded by the smoke.

On the southern bank, further down river, the fire situation at the Royal Arsenal at Woolwich was just as bad. Buildings here had been badly hit by the first wave of bombers and, as at Surrey Docks, there were several out-of-control fires within the vast area of the munitions factory. Crews from both land and river units found that as they laid out more and more lines of hose from their pumps, they were faced with the additional hazards of exploding projectiles flying through the air as fire reached standing ammunition dumps. Many of the buildings on fire contained live rounds and large quantities of nitro-glycerine. At the Royal Arsenal and at the Surrey Docks, high-explosive bombing had damaged water mains and many fire hydrants were dry. Fortunately fireboats, by lying some way off, were able to pump up to 4 tons of water a minute from the Thames to those ashore, but wherever possible use was made of alternative supplies, including static dams, dykes and even ditches on neighbouring marsh-land. By 8.15pm over half a square mile of fire was reported.

A quarter of an hour later, with the second air-raid of the night seemingly incessant overhead, Lambeth Regional Control asked Number Six Region, comprising the Thames Valley and South Midlands, to begin moving its units into holding positions on the outer fringes of north and east London. As they began to arrive these men and pumps were dispatched to the City of London area where several major outbreaks around the Barbican had been reported and initial reconnaissance indicated that more manpower and machines were urgently required.

In the Silvertown district of West Ham, great raging fires

blocked most road exits from the region and for a while some civilians were evacuated by boats to safer places further along the Thames. The movement of men and equipment continued during the unabating air attack but was, in many cases, aggravated by the breakdown in telephone communications. The central fire service mobilising control for the West Ham area was housed in a school. Since the early hours of the first raid, damage to telephone links was such that all orders for appliance movement were carried by AFS dispatch riders. Aside from the 500 LFS pumps sent to West Ham, many of the London dispatch riders were also busy carrying messages between the officers-in-charge of the numerous fires around the Royal Docks.

Air-raids continued intermittently, with a sharp incendiary-bomb attack being delivered to Old Kent Road just before 2am. While London Regional Control was hastily mustering enough pumps to deal with this threat, another major fire occurred as heavy bombing hit Woodford on the north-east border of the region, demanding even more of the available resources. Most pumps sent to these two incidents were drawn from supporting Home County regions, whose crews were now arriving in London and being deployed to fires in some strength. From midnight onwards, the whole of the regular and AFS capacity of the LFS was at work, scattered widely across the eastern and central parts of the capital, and right down to its southern borders.

THE GREAT FIRE OVER AGAIN

The Thames, with its riverside fires, created a spectacle probably unmatched since the Great Fire of 1666. Parts of the southern warehouse frontage below Tower Bridge were alight for over 1,000 yards—one continuous wall of fire. Many moored vessels were ablaze from end to end, and numerous burning 100-ton dumb barges, whose moorings had burned through, drifted down river with the ebbing tide

79

like funeral pyres, endangering other craft and riverside buildings. A convoy of six fireboats which had been ordered back to London from the Thameshaven fires, came up to Woolwich Reach just before midnight. The officer commanding this small flotilla described the scene:

We kept close formation until we reached Woolwich, and then we saw an extraordinary spectacle. There was nothing but fire ahead, apparently stretching right across the river and burning on both its banks. We seemed to be entering a tunnel of fire— no break in it anywhere. All the usual landmarks were obliterated by walls of flame. Burning barges drifted past. For many hours no contact with the shore was possible. We did what we could where we could as we slowly worked our way up river.

At one time we were just getting into position to fight a fire in a large warehouse when the whole of the riverside front collapsed into the water with a mighty splash. The contents of the building, bags of beans, pouring into the river made a sound like a tropical rain storm. Soon after, we were surprised to see two firemen and three firewomen picking their way along the shore in the direction of Southwark Bridge; they told us they had been cut off in a control room for several hours. They had undoubtedly had a rough time of it, but did not seem unduly perturbed.

Often, warehouse fires posed additional problems because of their contents. At one inferno in Bermondsey the air was heavy with pepper and firemen found breathing an unpleasant and difficult task in itself. There were paint fires, sugar fires and tea fires. At a dockside building full of grain, rats poured out in a steady stream to escape the fire and thick smoke inside.

An AFS fireman on his first real night of action at Rum Wharf, East India Docks, later said:

... The fires had a stunning effect. Wherever the eye could see, vast sheets of flame and a terrific roar. It was so bright there was no need for headlights.
... The first line of warehouses was ablaze from end to end ...
I walked down between the two warehouses myself. Half-way

down was a staff car in the middle of the causeway. Standing nonchalantly by it was a young WAFS, outwardly not taking a blind bit of notice of the stuff that was falling pretty thick all around. Seeing her I strolled past as if I was used to walking out in the middle of falling bombs every Saturday afternoon. We gave each other a sickly smile and I passed on . . .

The fire was so huge that we could do little more than make a feeble attempt to put it out. The whole of that warehouse was a raging inferno, against which were silhouetted groups of pigmy firemen directing their futile jets at the wall of flame . . . While we were working on our branch—we had to keep in the same position for hours on end, unable to let go of the branch to take cover when bombs fell—a large cargo ship took fire for'ard . . . We put this fire out in half an hour and then returned to our warehouse.

In spite of the numbness, you have time to think a little while you crouch over the branch and I remembered the crowd of women and children whom we had met as we rode in, streaming away from the danger area, carrying bundles over their shoulders. Some would run out into the roadway and call to us to come and attend to their fires . . .

Occasionally we would glance up and then we would see a strange sight, for a flock of pigeons kept circling round overhead almost all night. They seemed lost, as if they couldn't understand the unnatural dawn. It looked like sunrise all round us. The pigeons seemed white in the glare, birds of peace making a strange contrast with the scene below.

From 3am onwards, however, came the first indications that some measure of control was being achieved over the numerous fires and the repeated calls for petrol, oil and basic refreshments started to be met. Relief for the crews that had been at work since 5pm the previous afternoon was a priority, and by the time that the 'all clear' sounded across eastern London just before five o'clock, some semblance of fire service organisation was apparent. Most of the major fires were coming under control. Fresh crews from Number Twelve Region began to arrive in large numbers and from the first canteen vehicles women AFS members started to dispense hot drinks and sandwiches to crews as they were relieved at the larger incidents, such as at the Surrey Docks. London control had logged over 1,000 fire calls by 4am although with the number of incendiaries falling throughout the night, it was obvious that many small fires had been unattended in their earlier stages; consequently they grew and merged with the next nearest blaze. During the height of the night's activity many crews turned out to a street address only to find half a dozen fires to choose from.

As dawn rose over London, it revealed a scene around the docks area of a still smoking and steaming devastation. Partially collapsed buildings, many still burning deep down in the impacted debris, gutted and charred shells, were all that remained of the majority of streets. Some premises had fallen down and blocked roads. Glass, bricks and splintered woodwork lay all around. A number of appliances still pumping were isolated by buildings that had collapsed on either side of them. A fog of pungent smoke hung low over the riverside district and eddied around as each relief fire appliance drove up. In the docks and river basins, over sixty vessels had been sunk and many more damaged by fire. During those long hours of 7–8 September 1940, 430 men, women and children were killed, mostly by the blasts from high-explosive bombs. Seven firemen were dead and many injured, some seriously.

At Lambeth Headquarters, Major Jackson decided that with the grave risk of resumed raiding at nightfall, *all* personnel were to remain on continuous duty until further notice. As the capital's population began to emerge from their shelters to observe the carnage and damage, work went on to subdue the remaining fires. A lot of the men on the off-duty watch had reported for work during the raid and they, along with the relief crews, were able to begin recovering pumps and making up hose and equipment, much of it filthy and damaged by falling masonry or pierced by flying glass. The task was a mammoth one, with men almost asleep on their feet, leaning against branch-holders or slumped over the controls of pumps. They had worked non-stop for more than ten hours in sodden uniforms and were ravenously hungry, yet the spirits of the auxiliaries could not have been higher.

Whilst the damping-down and clearing-up operations got under way that morning, AFS personnel knew they had withstood the bombing and braved some of the worst fires London had ever seen. They had trained and trained, and their waiting had lasted more than a year. On this morning, despite the tremendous damage, theirs was a kind of victory.

At the scenes of the larger fires, crews were released as fresh manpower became available. Here much hose and other equipment was still in use and left in position. Those firemen clearing up had a hard task of rolling up unco-operative 75ft lengths of hose, most of which were semi-rigid after having withstood great pressures of water for hours on end. The hose seemed to roll up in a series of uncompromising right angles, finishing up an unwieldy, heavy and almost square bundle. Hundreds of such lengths had to be made up and conveyed back to fire stations to be unrolled, scrubbed, checked, tested and hung up to dry. Pumps had to be restocked with what dry hose was available. Much of this work was carried out at AFS sub-stations by crews working in their under-clothes, for having only one uniform suddenly took on a new dimension. All over AFS stations, clustering over any source of heat such as hot-water pipes, and even the bonnets of pumps still warm from the night's marathon, were rows and rows of dripping fire tunics. Most were still wet by mid-afternoon, by which time the men had eaten a hot meal in between the re-stowing of gear. Some even managed a little rest on beds or palliasses or on fire-station floors, exhausted minds and bodies seeking a little solace; sleep was about to become a precious commodity for the London fire-fighters. Future nights were to bring officers, men and women, closer to their foe than they could have ever imagined, demanding a superhuman effort from them all.

As if to show that London's firemen and women could take a night like that in their stride, an entry in the brigade's official War Diary, kept at headquarters, read quite simply:

September 7/8 1940:
    A big raid caused great fires at Surrey Docks, East and West India Docks and the Royal Arsenal, which taxed the whole of the LFS.

This was an understatement of the true magnitude of the fires fought that night, but there were even greater battles against fire yet to come. Immediately ahead lay fifty-six consecutive nights of unrelenting pyrotechnic hell for London.

5

The Relentless Raids

During the massive clearing-up and damping-down operations on the morning of 8 September, Jackson and his senior
officers at LFB Headquarters were able for the first time to
take stock of the situation. Uppermost in their minds was the
likelihood of further raids, possibly even during daylight as
the first of the previous day's had been. Jackson recognised
that the fire-fighters' problems identified during the raids
were not going to be solved at one stroke, for they encom-
passed such things as lack of adequate communications, a
severe shortage of water from mains damaged by high explosives, and no proper chain of command at some of the major
fires. Solutions to the new pressures of fire-fighting under
such difficult and dangerous conditions were not easily
found. Bombing had caused early damage to telephone links,
and collapsed buildings made the dispatch riders' task a
hazardous one, especially at night under shaded lighting.

Jackson's officers were few in relation to the huge numbers
of fires the night before and it looked as if the senior AFS firemen were going occasionally to find themselves in the awesome
position of commanding a crew at a fire of near-conflagration
proportions; it was also clear that the damage to water mains
and fire hydrants was another matter that the LFS was simply
going to have to live with. In a way it was fortunate that the
Thames area had been the centrepiece of the night's raids, as
a fair quantity of water had been constantly available from
the river itself, which despite its tidal fluctuations had been at
a reasonable level. Even so, getting the necessary lines of hose
ashore from fireboats had proved no easy task, and certainly

one that could not be achieved in a few minutes.

OVERALL STRATEGY

A more important subject to concern Jackson and his staff that morning was the consideration of the need for a whole change of strategy towards air-raid fire-fighting. During the previous night, there had been an attempt to view each large fire separately, as would have been the case in peacetime. Now it was clearly going to be a matter of regional headquarters monitoring the *overall* fire situation in the London area and deploying available resources accordingly, with the whole position in mind. It was also plain to many regular LFB men, that the high standards of peacetime fire-fighting were going to be useless in coping with air-raid fires. The pre-war days of close-range operating, with firemen working their way deep inside a smoke-filled building to fight the fiery enemy at close quarters, were soon to be faded memories. The blitz fires needed plenty of water through powerful jets which in peacetime would have meant tremendous water damage to the fabric and contents of any structure involved in fire. Indeed, the hallmark of the LFB had been its ability to rapidly get stuck into a situation and bring it under control using the minimum amount of water. But overnight, and in spite of some local shortages, thousands of jets of water had been aimed into blazing premises across London as both LFB regulars and AFS crews quickly realised a desperate situation demanded a desperate attack. On the first day several million gallons of water had been used at the dock fires alone.

On the afternoon of 8 September, as those lucky enough to snatch some rest dozed whilst their steaming uniforms began to dry out, there were two air-raid alerts although both were cancelled within half an hour. No enemy aircraft appeared over the region. As was the practice, all duty crews were 'stood to' during these periods and the men waiting alongside their pumps must have been apprehensive as to

Two firemen lean into the reaction of a powerful jet – Lipton's Tea Warehouse, Shoreditch, East London. Photograph taken solely by the light from the fire. 11 December 1940 (*Daily Mirror*)

One of Wren's churches takes fire – St Bride, Fleet Street, with flames breaking out around the clock face and above. 29 December 1940 (*Daily Mirror*)

what the early evening and night would bring. Intelligence reports showed that the Luftwaffe was now in occupation of French coastal airfields. At seven o'clock in the evening, the first squadrons of heavily laden Heinkels and Dorniers roared down runways, lifted off and set course for the second night running towards the clear line of the Thames and then the capital. The sirens sounded in London just before 8pm. Fifteen minutes later, most London fire stations were again devoid of crews and appliances, leaving a few firewomen manning telephones in the watchrooms co-ordinating the transient dispatch riders.

Again, it was the docks that first received the full force of the incendiary attack from 200 aircraft and it soon became apparent that the following waves of bombers were deliberately aiming at the larger fires. Hundreds of incendiaries caused a major fire area at Old Change, near St Paul's Cathedral, and there was another potential conflagration at Woolwich Arsenal. Reports of the severity of the situation near St Paul's led the Prime Minister himself to express concern, but Commander Firebrace was able to reassure Mr Churchill that all was under control. First reconnaissance of the Woolwich Arsenal told of: 'A square mile of danger, buildings laden with high-explosive shells well alight and spreading . . .'

Before the raid was an hour old, Jackson was asking Firebrace's staff at Home Office Control for urgent support from outside the London region. Within the next half-hour, reinforcements were sent to London from as far away as Birmingham, East Anglia and the West Country. The raid lasted sporadically until 5am the following morning, and like the night of 7 September, set the pattern of life for the LFS for the next fifty-five nights. Huge fires again raged from the City to West Ham and amongst the first fire service buildings to be hit by high explosives was Whitechapel Fire Station in Commercial Road, E1, causing several LFB casualties including firewomen.

SEPTEMBER NIGHT

Philip Henderson had worked in Fleet Street for some years and moved into a literary career before the outbreak of war. He had joined Marlow, Buckinghamshire, AFS but transferred to London in the spring of 1940. He recalled this September night:

> The call comes through fairly early in the evening. I have, in fact, only just put on my boots and leggings when the bells go down and all pumps are ordered to West Ham.
>
> From the sound of things we know we are in for a bad night, and as we drive in convoy through the East End we soon run into the unnatural day made by scores of fires. Far up barrage balloons float like silver toys in the light of an angry sunset. Volumes of vivid smoke pour up from factories and warehouses; showers of sparks tossed from the housetops fly towards us like a swarm of yellow bees; even the road is alight with the whitish-green of newly fallen incendiaries. Overhead flares float down, breaking up and melting as they fall into the glare of their own gigantic candlelight. But still groups of men stand in doorways watching this evil firework display provided for them by the Luftwaffe.
>
> Just then two bombs, ripping their way through the air in rapid succession, pass overhead and land in the middle of a great fire on our left. We try to flatten ourselves against the sides of the tender, while debris and shrapnel rain down in all directions. But, unbelievably, the pump behind us is still following; the third is lost to sight. As usual, what with bomb craters, roads blocked by collapsed houses and burst water-mains, the driver loses his way. We circle in and out of blasted streets of little houses, their window frames hanging loose, their walls pitted white with shrapnel as though they have been visited by some disastrous plague. Then wide flashes and the explosions of still more bombs. Close by an incendiary is lodged, burning dangerously, on top of a gasometer.
>
> Victoria Dock itself is brilliant with yellow flame, lighting up the funnels and masts of ships and an immense drifting pall of white smoke. It seems hopeless even to try to deal with such fires and the thought of what excellent targets they make from the air adds to the general feeling of impotence.
>
> Our three pumps and heavy unit draw alongside a railway line

with its forlorn little station. Bombs are still falling and flares slowly floating down. There is an odd popping sound as two lines of puce-coloured bullets follow one another up into the sky. The fence dividing the line from the road has been blown down, and as we are feverishly clearing the planks away I tear my hand on a nail. The pump-man has already set into a small canal, and we begin running out lines of hose into a yard where some rolls of coconut-matting are burning against the wall of a house. In the middle of the yard a lorry is burning like something in a dream. Then our water is hissing and thudding against it and we are staggering about with the pressure.

A thin jet is wavering up through the window cavity of a large warehouse, now simply a crimson shell of fire. The front of the adjacent building has already collapsed into the street. Next door three men are grouped round a branch in front of a burning row of small one-storeyed houses. A little sub-officer in his black coxcomb helmet is walking up and down, waving his arms, shouting commands.

'A drop in here.' The men swing the long hissing jet over to the next house. 'Now give this one a drink.' The jet wavers, leaping and splashing fiercely against the outside wall, fumbling its way to the smoking cavity of a window. 'Another drop in this one,' shouts the little sub-officer.

Across the railway line the roof of a house is burning furiously. We begin running out hose over the lines. Two men get to work from the street level and another man and myself direct our jet from a bridge in the middle of the line. Get the roof covered with a blanket of smoke, I think, and it won't make such a good target. But 'they' have seen it, of course, and great fanlike flashes spring up from the next street; their explosions violently shake the bridge and there is a rush of warm air and the frightening smell of cordite.

'Blimey! Those were near ones!' remarks my companion, an old sergeant from the last war.

Far up a plane is whining into a dive. AA guns let fly at it, and the evil throbbing, like the throbbing insistence of pain, grows fainter. A lone searchlight is moving slowly across the sky. Then the antidote of gunfire wears off again, the pain in the sore red sky returns, and we think that the next bombs must surely hit our bridge. Already wet and shivering with cold, I feel that I am going to be sick, but can't duck or let go of the branch or the pressure will send it flying back and knock our brains out. The only thing to do is hold on, though my arms are breaking with cramp and all feeling has gone out of my hands, hold on and stand waiting for the next bomb to fall on us.

'You're not nervous, are you?' asks my companion by way of reassurance. I am trembling uncontrollably and giving vent to faint groans. The pain in my arms is becoming unbearable. 'You're all right, lad! You're all right. Just hold on. Don't let go, for Christ's sake!'

Half stupefied, I ask: 'What shall we do if a bomb hits the bridge? Drop the branch?'

'Well . . .' He gives a snort of laughter. 'We shan't have much time . . .'

A red flash followed by a sharp, vicious report leaps up almost next-door to our burning house. They are certainly bombing our fire. Then, in quick succession, more flashes and explosions. I am surprised not to hear the descent of these bombs. It is as though red globes suddenly appeared from nowhere and burst into the houses themselves, reminding me of William Blake's drawing of hell in which a human heart is plunged into a bowl of fire.

'Isn't there any chance of a relief?'

'No, we'll have to hold on for another three hours yet at least.'

I am not sure whether he is joking or not. But soon after that our station officer comes round. It is his first night out in the blitz, and he seems quite bewildered. This kind of thing is not accounted for in General Orders. He says he will tell the pump man to knock off and we can have a rest and a smoke.

A smoke? I had been standing with my hands on a level with my head, steadying the branch against the top of the bridge, and as soon as I let go and the blood begins to circulate freely again, all I can do is dance about with pain. My companion has gone, but the droning planes are there again, shells are bursting blindly and clumsily overhead and the next thing is the bombs. This time I am free to crouch down behind the iron of the bridge. They fall farther off. The sky still looks red and sore, a searchlight is probing the wound, but the general glare of the fires seems to have died down and the roof upon which we had been directing our jet is now only a black skeleton.

As can be seen from this account, the burden upon the LFB officers of trying to control the fires widely scattered across the capital, was an immense one. Four divisional officers and seven superintendents, backed up by eleven district officers, went from fire to fire in staff cars mostly driven by AFS firewomen in an endeavour to co-ordinate operations. During the early days of the war, appliance mobilisation arrangements at principal stations had been the province of LFB regular officers, but these important duties were now given to AFS women to allow more officers to get out into the action. The firewomen, in fact, more than proved their ability to cope with these tasks, and for the remainder of the war continued to staff the major control rooms of the LFS.

Major Jackson himself took off from his Lambeth HQ to view some of the worst nights' fires and offer a few words of encouragement to the hard-pressed crews; yet he was back at his desk at 9am trying to deal with the problems of the 30,000 men and women directly under his command.

That morning (9 September) the overall fire situation broadly resembled that following the previous day's raids. The last of the major fires at London Docks was coming under control. All other fires were either being finally damped down or had literally burned themselves out, as many small island sites did. These latter cases only subsided when there was nothing left for the flames to consume, when their awesome energy gradually diminished in intensity and finally went out. Large piles of hot ash and scorched girders would mark where buildings had once stood. A real problem was that small fires went undetected in their early stages. Even officers of the Metropolitan Police had clear instructions to take cover whilst a raid was in progress, and but for firemen and wardens the streets were deserted.

Relief crews from outside London began to be available to relieve the weary and bedraggled firemen still tending their pumps and directing jets of water. Thus the pattern was set for London's fire-fighters. From early September 1940 onwards, the Luftwaffe came to bomb the capital with deadly fire loads every night, right through until 3 November.

Almost without fail, the first bombs would fall at around 8pm and the raid would continue until 5am the next morning. Generally every fire was under control by the dawn, although the prolonged and exhaustive damping-down and clearing-up operations of the daytime practically merged with the first 'red' air-raid alert of the following evening. In the first crucial minutes of a raid, many crews would respond and go to a building they had striven hard to save the night before, to find it ablaze from end to end yet again.

LOCAL BOYS MAKE GOOD

Yet the morale of the LFS was now at its highest level for, from 8 September onwards, the public attitude towards them began to change. Grimy and weary crews driving homeward to their stations, found that they were constantly cheered by pedestrians. After a year of continually standing to and waiting, these moments must have been sweet for the AFS men and women. The Thameshaven oil-fire battles had been fought with almost no spectators to witness the struggle. But on this September morning, as the populations of West and East Ham, Silvertown, Rotherhithe, Poplar and other London districts emerged and made their way to work as best they could, they could see the aftermath of exactly what London's firemen had had to face.

Michael Wassey recalled a typical civilian comment of this time: 'Blimey, army dodgers! It's ridiculous! I'll admit I used to laugh at them a bit myself. Not now, though. I saw one lot go down like ninepins. Their engine went up, though. The AFS and the regular firemen, they were all magnificent, just bloody well magnificent.'

Cinema audiences openly applauded firemen on newsreels and complete strangers stood them rounds of drinks in pubs. National and local newspapers made much of the fire-fighting 'heroes'; as the Luftwaffe came nightly to pour more fire and explosives over the London region there could hardly have

been any one on the home front who did not warm enthusiastically to the achievements of both the AFS firemen and the
regular crews. A *Daily Mirror* Zec double cartoon of 14 September 1940, entitled 'Local Boys Make Good', probably
made its point better than most, showing a 1939 AFS fireman
(and ARP warden) dodging the bricks. The same 1940 duo
were shown being showered with flowers.

Despite this long-overdue recognition, London firemen
continued to face both the most overwhelming odds and
occasionally a personal horror. AFS Fireman Vic Flint's diary
graphically recalls such a moment during the night of 12
September, when he was at a huge fire in London Docks:

> I can remember the *Massey Shaw* (the fire brigade river boat)
> coming alongside the dock, and I can remember a Molotov
> breaking up right over the job. I picked up some of the incen-
> diaries with my hands (by the unburnt portion) and threw them
> into the dock. I can remember, too, the sight of Macawley
> (he's from 16) lying in the gutter with one of his legs off and
> the water from the fire running over his face, so that I thought
> he would be drowned.
>
> After I saw Macawley, God was I frightened? Somehow the
> sight of a man you've known lying there with his leg off and
> the water running over him and nobody doing anything about
> it, puts the wind up you. I have always thought that 'knees
> knocking together' was just a phrase, but my knees did literally
> knock together—I could feel them. And then Adams told me to
> get up the ladder and put some water into the warehouse. So
> up I went.

WEAPONS, COUNTER-WEAPONS—AND WATER

The incendiaries dropped by the Luftwaffe were primarily
of a thermite type, cylindrical, about 18in long and weighing
approximately a kilo. They had an impact-fuse device which
caused the magnesium alloy case of the bomb itself to burn
furiously. As the nightly raids continued, a similar type of
incendiary was dropped that had a small time-delay explosive
device. The other kind of fire invention used at this time was

the oil bomb. About the size of a dustbin, these took fire on impact with the ground or a roof, flinging out flaming oil and metal splinters all around. During late September, yet another variation on the high-explosive theme was introduced by the enemy. These were parachute mines which floated down and then fused their deadly charge. However, they became particularly hazardous when they fell into the soft mud at the edge of the Thames during low tide or into the water of a dock basin. Then they became magnetic mines and lay ready to detonate upon the passing of any fireboats, especially when these craft were putting lines of hose to pumps ashore.

A variety of situations continued to test the growing confidence of the fire-fighters. On the night of 12 September, an oil bomb crashed through the roof of the peers' record room in the House of Lords, but damage was confined to the room by LFS personnel stationed permanently in the Palace of Westminster. Three nights later, an enemy bomber shot down by a fighter aircraft fell into the forecourt of Victoria Railway Station. Sadly, the RAF plane that had scored this victory was also damaged and crashed nearby.

All through these nights it was a story of the battle for water. Moving vast quantities from one relatively unaffected area to a fire zone was the key to the firemen's victory; but a weakness in overall fire-fighting strategy was that it relied heavily on public water mains, which were easily damaged and shattered by high-explosive bombing. Even when large trunk water supplies were unaffected (which was rare), over one hundred pumps at work from such a source could quickly completely absorb the capacity of the water main. The 5,000-gallon street dams only provided one pumping appliance with enough water to produce two good fire-fighting jets for about ten minutes, and many fires required hours of a barrage-type attack.

Under the conditions which prevailed during those first September night raids, the hose lorries and water units really came into their own, although the miles of large-diameter hoses they were able to lay through the streets were vulnerable to falling walls, metal and glass splinters and red-hot debris. Much of this hose was useless before any water could be fed through from a distant pump. Even if a water relay did survive the bombs, there were often problems caused by ill-trained pump operators—with a long relay it became necessary to interpose pumps at intervals along the hose line, just to keep the pressure up and the quantities of sorely needed water moving. This was a very delicate operation requiring fine judgement and constant reading of pump gauges and throttle settings. Burst lengths of hose and a failed relay bore testimony to an inexperienced operator.

The numerous roof fires meant continual mobilising of every turntable ladder (TLs) in the region, as in most cases it was only possible for firemen to gain quick access via these 100ft ladders to the rapidly growing flames on uppermost parts of buildings. Further TLs were being commissioned and placed in action to supplement London's existing fleet of such appliances.

Besides the constant failure of fire hydrants owing to bomb damage to water mains, the high explosives also ruptured gas mains causing leaks, which were yet another source of fires in the streets above. These gas fires usually occurred in bomb craters or just above the surface of a street, where their tell-tale blue flames indicated the source of the fire. Gas fires were normally allowed to burn until the gas workers were able to seal off the broken main. Such incidents were a perpetual nuisance to firemen, and were dealt with by using large quantities of damp clay as an effective sealer.

By the middle of September, the previously raw AFS firemen had added immeasurably to their blitz experience; during the previous year, it would have been hard to predict the general esteem in which they were held by 1940. The Home Secretary, Sir John Anderson, sent a special message to the men and women of the London Fire Service:

... though it might seem invidious to draw distinctions in the Civil Defence Services, no one would begrudge a special word of commendation to the Fire Service and its dauntless courage and many casualties.

In the run-up to war, the LFB had sensibly recognised the potential value of several existing 'works fire brigades'. These were fire-fighting units established by industrial and commercial concerns to operate within the boundaries of large factory complexes or riverside wharf areas. They usually consisted of a small number of trained and enthusiastic employees who were able to provide swift fire cover. A number of works brigades were equipped at the outbreak of war with trailer pumps and lengths of hose to supplement their existing fire-fighting capacity. Once the blitz started, the works brigades tackled unaided some large fires on their own premises; rarely was the LFS able to supplement their admirable efforts.

NIGHT AFTER DAY AFTER NIGHT

On successive nights of raiding in September, the target areas gradually grew wider and the West End began to receive a share of the treatment that had previously been meted out to East London. Brief entries in the LFB war diary for the period 10–16 September read:

Tenth:
   A determined attack at St Katharine's and London Docks. Numerous large fires.
Eleventh:
   Great anti-aircraft barrage started. Eighteen large fires with one in Lambeth involving sixteen small factories. Some lives again lost by bombing and shrapnel but morale improved by our AA fire.
Twelfth:
   Heavy bombing in Belsize, Hampstead and Fulham. Fires, although numerous, were small and only two—the Western Fever Hospital and the Church of Our Lady of Victory, Ken-

sington, requiring twenty pumps' attendance. Later calls fairly light but a thirty pump incident occurred in Westminster Bridge Road. Plumstead sub-station hit by bomb and two men and one woman auxiliary killed and several injured.

Thirteenth:

Afternoon raid resulted in small number of minor fires, only two, (one in Scotland Yard) being serious. During the night ten fires classed as serious and one major. Sub-station at Abbey Choir School, Westminster, suffered direct hit and four men injured. An escape-ladder unit attached to a Battersea sub-station wrecked by bomb. Delayed action bomb exploded outside Buckingham Palace.

Fourteenth:

High explosive bombing of St Thomas's Hospital necessitated twenty pump attendance. North and east blocks of Southwark Fire Station hit by high explosives but no casualties. Brixton, Clapham and Balham received heaviest bombing. 230 small fires reported in that area as well as five serious incidents. Later in the night major fires at Shadwell and in the Old Kent Road.

Sixteenth:

Nearly 700 fires logged during the night. Bombing very severe in the City, Central, Northern, Eastern and South Eastern districts. Sixteen serious and three major fires in these areas.

And so it went on, night merging into day, into night, week and month. On 16 September, Major Jackson was able to present a brief report to the London County Council Civil Defence Committee, in which he broadly described the results of the previous weeks' raiding. He told of a casualty list so far of 2 officers, 19 firemen and 1 woman auxiliary killed; 31 regular LFB men, 120 men auxiliaries, 3 women and 1 youth seriously injured; 11 auxiliaries were missing, presumed dead. Three LFB fire stations, Whitechapel, Southwark, and Euston Road had been hit and eighteen sub-stations damaged beyond occupation. Jackson also reported that as the fires were being controlled by morning, and a certain amount of military assistance had been available for clearing-up operations during daytime hours, he was relaxing the continuous-duty system back to shift working—forty-eight

hours on, twenty-four hours off. He was not, however, allow-
ing any other leave.

Two unusual, separate incidents of this period illustrate
the harsh reality of fire-fighting in the face of falling bombs.
The first took place during the initial raid of 7 September.
Whilst a fire was in progress in Peckham, South London, a
high-explosive bomb fell in Bonar Road, right under the
tailboard of an LFS hose-laying lorry which had been parked
well clear of operations. The lorry and its driver literally
disappeared. Some three days later, when a lull in raiding
permitted some repair work to the damaged terraced houses
in the vicinity, a repair party found some hose amid the
debris of a partially collapsed house. Peckham Fire Station
was informed and a crew went to the scene in an attempt to
retrieve the hose. When they arrived and scouted around the
building, they found not only more hose under the bricks and
timber, but the missing hose lorry itself firmly embedded in
the roof structure and upper floor of the house. It was in a
position where it was completely concealed from view from
the street. The vehicle was remarkably intact considering
that it had been projected over 100ft through the air by bomb
blast. Most of the hose that had been carried by the lorry was
subsequently recovered and put into use again. No trace was
ever found of the AFS driver.

The second incident involved the two-man crew of a
turntable ladder which was at work as a water tower, projecting a water jet on to a range of roof fires in Great Portland
Street, W1, on 18 September. The ladder was fully extended
to 100ft and the fireman at the top was about to secure himself
to the ladder by a safety belt when a bomb whistled down past
him and blew up in the street directly below. There the second
fireman of the crew was operating the ladder controls; he
and an officer standing close by were severely wounded—the
latter died later that night. But the fireman at the ladder top
had an amazing escape. When the bomb burst, the chassis of
the turntable ladder was blown sideways into the front of the

building, but the rear wheel, axle and ladder base section, collectively weighing over 4 tons, was blown right over the rooftop and came crashing to rest on another roof nearby. Various steel sections of the ladder were thrown on to the roof also, but the uppermost ladder extension caught on a projection, turned over through 360° and hung down over the front of the building which was still on fire. The unfortunate fireman who had been at the top of the ladder was thrown into the air, then fell to the pavement to be buried by falling debris. When the dust had settled, a search was mounted in the area and this fireman was found still alive but seriously injured. After months of hospital treatment, he survived the war and although disabled, was able to run a public house in King's Cross, not far from the scene of this incredible escape.

A singular act of fire service bravery occurred on 17 September 1940. Auxiliary Fireman Harry Errington was on duty at Rathbone Street sub-station, W1, just off Oxford Street, when the premises were virtually demolished by a direct hit. Seven AFS personnel were killed outright but three others, including Errington, were injured and trapped in the basement. Fire broke out in the debris beneath which the two other firemen were trapped. Despite his own injuries, Errington was able to extricate both men and carry them out to safety and in doing so suffered extensive burns himself. For his extreme courage, Errington was awarded the George Cross. Unfortunately, the honour of this award was soured by the shabby treatment which Errington received under the existing Civil Injuries Act that applied to the fire service: this ruled that men injured in war service could only be kept on at full pay for thirteen weeks. Errington's burns failed to heal in this period and he was compulsorily discharged from the LFS.

As September wore on into October 1940, the persistent nightly raids continued. There was little respite for the fire-fighters. Jack Read had been in advertising before joining

the AFS in 1938 and served at Lambeth. He recalled a night
duty during this period when his crew were sent to a hospital
blaze:

This is a bigger job as there are already crews working there.
Jerry is still active as we drive to the hospital. We can hear a
bomb and then another swish down and explode. We all duck
down as low as possible in our appliances. Not that it's any good
ducking down in an appliance, but it makes you feel a bit more
secure. The bombs explode a good way off, but they always
sound so darned close while they are falling. The only useful
thing about the fires is that they illuminate the roads. We drive
pretty fast towards the hospital. We pass one or two ambulances
and a rescue squad going on to their assignments before we
arrive at the hospital. This is the busiest night I have had since
the docks went up in flames way back in September. It's better
now than it was then. Now we have AA guns. They don't bring
down many Jerries, but they sound good in spite of the nasty
little bits of steel that come down. You have a feeling that Jerry
is not getting it all his own way. Then in September we were
raw at practical fire-fighting, but now most feel more confident
about what to do and when to do it.

At the hospital I leave my crew at the main gates and go off
to find the officer-in-charge of the fire. I am told that he is up
on the roof, so I walk up three flights of stairs and then up an
outside iron ladder to reach him. He is standing in the middle of
the small bridge that connects the two top floors of opposite
wings of the hospital. I recognise him by his brass epaulettes.
His face is black with wood ash. I report the presence of my
crew, but we are not wanted as the fire is well under control.
Before I am dismissed I am told to assist the officer to pay out a
little more hose so that the men on the roof can get closer to the
remaining fire. The hose comes from a heavy pump that is
working from a water dam on the ground about thirty feet
from where we are standing. It is charged with water, and
three of us have to pull hard to get the extra foot or so that the
roof men need. I can hear Jerry flying around still, and from my
high position I can see a number of fires burning. It certainly is
a stinker tonight, but the glow from the fires is getting dull.

Then without any warning, without any whistle or swish, a
high explosive bomb drops on the ground underneath our
bridge. I am hurled upwards through the air at a terrifying

speed. At the top of my flight I seem to be stationary for a second. I am conscious of a brilliant light from the exploding bomb, and in this instant I see the bridge breaking up underneath me. Kirby, the officer-in-charge, is flying through the air, and the light is playing on his polished brass epaulettes. There is the roar of the explosion and the rumble of falling bricks and masonry. Then it is dark. I begin to turn over and over as I fall. I know that I have a long way to drop, and I imagine that I shall be killed when I reach the ground. I let my body go limp because I think that I will possibly avoid violent fractures. I wonder how much it is going to hurt. There is still a loud rumbling of falling debris and I feel my forehead become moist against the wind as something grazes the skin. It seems that I have already been falling a week. I begin to feel annoyed— annoyed at the thought of dying before this war is finished. A pattern of loosely connected thought impinges on my consciousness. All my life I have watched civilization in revolt: first creeping, then a stampede. It would have been so interesting, so exciting . . . to be able to beat down the forces that are trying to stop us . . . The future of mankind . . . A new and better world order . . . not by race domination. I might have seen the beginning of a world community . . . In our time, or in our children's time. In a small way I had hoped to be part of the great change, but here I am turning crazily over and over and falling towards my doom. I am annoyed. Then I realize that these feelings are stimulated by selfish motives, and I console myself that at least I have lived to see the turning point in civilization. That in itself is something. Then I wonder again how hard the ground is going to be.

I am conscious of the fact that I have stopped falling. There is a pain in my left arm, but I just can't think that I am alive. A piece of debris, a doorframe or something, lands across my chest, but its full force is taken by the debris that is on either side of me. I welcome the twinge in my chest. I must still be alive. I attempt to raise the debris, but my left arm will not respond to the impulse. My right arm is active, and I manage to get up and walk towards a group of dim lights that are approaching in front of me.

As I walk I hear a whimper and I look down on the ground. In the half-light I see the starched cuff of a nurse poking up out of a pile of rubble. The arm protrudes from the elbow, and the fingers move. I feel a bit sick inside. I say something about getting the nurse out and hope I sound confident. I scrape away at the bricks and the stench of mortar dust hangs in the air. Two men slide up behind me and fall into the job of excavating. I must have passed out then.

I am being carried along a corridor between a Home Guard and an orderly. I am delivered to two nurses who grin when they see me. They set about taking my clothes off and say that I look like a sweep. The nurses are magnificent. They get my heavy clothes off without causing much pain to my arm. I notice that my shoulder joint is somewhere between its normal position and my elbow. I am put into bed to wait for a doctor. The nurses make me feel that it's good to be alive, and they do not worry about two heavy bombs that fall close enough to send glass tinkling down outside. A doctor comes and gently lifts my arm back into its shoulder joint. It feels like Heaven now. Casualties are coming into the ward, and the cries of the wounded make me feel low. A nursing sister dies before the doctors can do anything for her. This sort of war is bloody. Kirby comes in from the operating theatre early in the morning with seventeen stitches across his head. I hear that he was buried at the bottom of the bomb crater for three hours, but while he was under the debris he managed somehow to tell an orderly to get a message to headquarters saying that the breakdown lorry and a crew were required to dig him and others out. The lorry arrived, and after the 'all clear' sounded they put on their floodlights and got the victims out. Kirby has got plenty of guts. I am told that Kirby and I are to be evacuated to Surrey in the morning. It will be nice down there.

A pal comes in to see me. He has been searching for me for hours. I can see he is glad to find me in bed alive. I go off to sleep after saying my prayers for the first time in years.

WAR WEARINESS

Even crews engaged in cooling-down operations found the going hard, and Auxiliary Fireman Charles Poulson, a pre-war cab driver, remembered going into a dockland job as one of a number of relief crews:

Now we turn off into a narrow, cobbled way, and on the left runs the high wall of the docks, blasted occasionally into tumble-down heaps of bricks.

A policeman and Home Guard appear like magic in the head-lights and wave us in.

It is apparent at once that we are in the docks. Outside, everything is dead and deserted, a lifeless empty city wrapped up in fear and darkness. But here, within these shattered walls, is bustle and activity. Huge ruddy piles glow everywhere. All the famed treasures of the docks and their huge storehouses are burning. Some scarlet in their intensity, shooting out flickering, fiery tongues, so vivid that it hurts the eyes to look; others sinking into a full defeated crimson.

Firemen are busy everywhere, and the place is a bedlam of roaring pumps, hissing water and falling roofs and walls. The very air is hot and heavy on the lungs, rotten with a thousand different stinks. And past it all the Thames flows on uncaring, its murky surface like burnished copper.

Through this red avenue we drive, bumping and banging over the lines of hose. Water under pressure makes them as hard as iron. Here, before us, is a towering structure of brown brick, its empty windows belching smoke. Hammet's Wharf! And before it on the river brink stands the pump we have come to relieve, roaring like an aeroplane. The operator leans against it, black and grimy from head to foot.

We pull up beside him and dismount.

'24 z?' asks Jim, as he's in charge.

The other, a tall brawny young man, nods wearily, as though past interest. The whites of his eyes shine out of his filthy, smoke-blackened face. Then he smiles politely, and his teeth show in a white flash.

'We're 38 w,' says Jim. 'We're relieving you.'

'It's about time.'

He seems to have had a hard time. That doesn't augur well for us.

'Been here long?' I ask.

'Well,' he replies, with delicate sarcasm, 'what day is it?'

Knowing exactly how he feels, we don't get annoyed. It's the old tale we all know so well on raidless nights—men left to work for a dozen hours at a time, while the reliefs loll in their stations and are not ordered on.

'Come on,' he says, 'I'll show you the job. It's well under now.'

We follow the two lines of snaky hose that run parallel from the pump into the doorway. I sniff the air.

'Hides?'

'And wool. And veneers. And soya beans. Full of oil; it'll blaze up all around you, if you let it.'

Now we enter the building. The fire has been fought and conquered, but is not yet dead. It is still full of hope, and lurks and smoulders between the piles and bales, under joists, in the walls, flaring up here and there, making sudden dashes and sallies. It must be fought relentlessly, until the burning stuff and debris have been turned over and doused and the constant streams of water have drowned the last hot ash. This is the process known as 'cooling down'.

As we pass the door, hacked off and hanging, our heads are enveloped in a great cloud of sickly yellow smoke, choking and acrid from the burning hides. We cough and stumble, eyes and noses streaming, and bend almost double. Here the air is at least breathable. Round our calves the water rushes on its way out.

The wooden partition walls have burned away or hang in shreds from the roof, making the whole interior one large hall. Everywhere lie piles of goods smouldering, or burnt and charred, sending up dense smoke, filling the place with a red lustre. Here and there flames are beginning to flicker out anew, though the water is inches deep. And out in the middle of this desolation, leaning wearily against the iron pillars, stooping low to breathe, stand the men we are to relieve, sending two glittering arcs of water hissing and thudding into the fires.

Auxiliary Vic Flint clearly underlined the overwhelming build-up of tiredness then being felt by the men and women of the LFS. He wrote:

It is strange when you are as exhausted as I am these days how little the opposite sex can mean to you. I came up the night before my leave ended, but when I got to London there was a heavy raid on. So I reported at 19 and they gave me a blanket on the floor of their control room. I went to sleep and when I woke up I found myself lying next to a very lovely blonde. She was one of the control room girls, and in our sleep we had moved into each other's arms for warmth. So we stayed like that for the rest of the night, but as far as I was concerned it didn't mean a thing.

I must be getting old, or something.

What a contrast to the lull before the blitz earlier in 1940, when the routine fifteen-minute start-up of taxi towing units disturbed many a nocturnal relationship on their comfortable rear seats!

NEAR-MISSES

Across London, fire-fighters continued to have narrow escapes from falling walls, lumps of masonry, flying metal and from bomb blast itself. On a night in late September, Auxiliary Fireman Frank Bartle was holding a high-pressure jet during the latter stages of operations following a large fire that had razed to the ground Kemble Bishops Barrel Store, at Bromley-by-Bow in East London. The occasional bomb was still falling and nearby, in the semi-darkness and flickering light from the dimming fire, was one of Frank's crew mates, Olly Goldsmith, who was also manning a jet. Frank suddenly heard a very loud metallic clang on the piles of bricks behind him but was unable to turn to see what the arrival was because he was holding the powerful jet. His immediate thought was that Olly, a renowned practical joker, was at work. Only days before, during a daytime purge on the cleanliness of Shoreditch sub-station before an inspection by a divisional officer, Olly had climbed to the roof of the school building and poured a bucket of water down a chimney. This did not improve the state of the scrubbed floor in the sub-station kitchen, minutes before the inspection started.

'Pack it up, Olly,' Frank called out into the darkness. 'I'm having a job to hold this bloody jet as it is.'

Olly did not reply and no more missiles arrived. Half an hour later, when the jet was shut down to allow for some repositioning, Frank turned and stumbled back across the debris towards the pump, only to come across a heavy cast-iron lamp post. This had caused the clang that he had heard when the lamp post had been sent flying as the result of a bomb blast in a street some distance away, being hurled over a nearby roof to this site.

By this stage of the blitz, most firemen had learnt enough about self-preservation to duck whenever possible upon hearing the whistle of a falling bomb. There is a story that illustrates this nicely. Alongside Moon's filling station in Commercial Road, only yards from Whitechapel Fire Station, was a coffee stall the proprietor of which was a redoubtable Jewish gentleman whose business had long flourished on this spot. He vowed that the Germans would not close his business down. During those occasional nights in September and October 1940, when the raiding was less intense in the area, he would keep the coffee stall open solely to attract the crews of pumps parked outside Whitechapel Fire Station whilst they waited for a call if a raid developed. On one such night, a large group of AFS firemen were crowded around the stall when suddenly came the high-pitched whistle of a descending bomb. All the firemen flattened themselves around the meagre protection of the wooden structure. The bomb exploded several streets away towards Mile End Road and rattled all the cups on the stall. To the surprise of the firemen, the gentleman behind his counter had continued to sort out his orders and stood smiling at the crouching firemen. 'What are you doing down there, boys?' he asked. 'Get on with your coffee.' Somewhat sheepishly, they got to their feet just as another whistle heralded a much closer bomb. To a man, the fire-fighters stayed upright as the explosion shook the stall again, but this time the coffee man had disappeared down behind his rows of mugs.

On another occasion, later on in the fifty-seven nights of continuous blitz, Auxiliary Fireman Frank Reader from a Shoreditch sub-station was driving an AFS pump to a large outbreak in St Leonard's Road, near to the north side of the Blackwall Tunnel. Finding his approach to this area blocked by a bomb crater, Frank turned the appliance and detoured via Burdett Road, Poplar. Whilst driving along, he suddenly noticed that he had company behind, for his vehicle was being followed by an LFB red pump. Just as Reader drove past the empty Burdett Road LFB station, there was a smattering of small hard fragments across the AFS appliance bonnet; then came an almighty 'crump' behind the speeding machine. Reader's crew on the back of the pump shouted and banged on the cab roof for him to stop. The entire steeple of a church had fallen out into the road *between* the two passing fire pumps. Fortunately the LFB machine was able to pull up in time to avoid serious damage to crew or appliance.

THE TARGETS WIDEN

In late September, the first statutory Fire Watchers' Order was made which required a person to be present to detect fire and summon assistance on premises where more than thirty people worked, in warehouses of more than 50,000 cubic feet, and in timber yards containing a similar amount of wood. In practice, it was clear to fire service personnel that this inadequate order was largely ignored and premises not covered by the order were just as flammable.

The LFB itself attempted to provide some sort of fire watch from those stations that had hose drying and drill towers high enough to command a view of the locality. These posts were manned by AFS firemen too old for operational duties and were equipped with a compass-type instrument able to give a bearing on any visible fire. The bearing was telephoned to Lambeth Headquarters and there located using cross bearings from other fire stations to give clear direction to the pumps being sent on.

Although the pattern of raids remained the same, the target areas continued to widen. On 24 September, of 740 fires as a result of bombing, over half were in the LFB 'A' district area, mainly London's West End. These included a 100 pump job in Southampton Buildings and large fires in Tottenham Court Road and Fleet Street. During that month

LFS pumps had been sent to Chiswick, Isleworth, Southall and Beckenham to assist the local crews of these brigades in coping with the aftermath of raids. By the first week of October 1940, four LFB fire stations and seven sub-stations had been hit and permanently put out of action; at all of them, fire service personnel, including AFS girls, had been casualties.

Quite suddenly, after a month of heavy non-stop night raiding, came a respite. On 6 October, only three fires were caused by Luftwaffe action, and although these were large incidents many crews had their first night in for weeks. It was not to last; the Heinkels and Dorniers were back in strength the next night and virtually all London fire stations were hard at it again.

Maurice Richardson, an AFS fireman at Soho Fire Station in central London, called it 'a time of cat-and-mouse rhythm'. Just when everybody felt that they had had as much of it as they could stand and that one more bad night would cause them to crack up, the pressure slackened. When they had recovered and were thinking that things were not so bad and they could stand it indefinitely—crash—down came a heavy load and they were out in it for two nights running.

There is little evidence that firemen or women wilted under the strain; indeed the majority seemed to flourish at this time. There even seemed to be an air of confidence about LFS ability to cope with what the next night's bombing would bring; as by now most London AFS men had seen and faced the most awful infernos, this was understandable.

In between the nights of perpetual raiding, an unusual task for firemen of the London region arose on 16 October, when they were required to bridge a 400yd gap in New River at Enfield, Middlesex. This was one of the capital's main water supplies and the gap resulted from enemy bombing, occurring at a time when there were serious shortages throughout London because of air-raid damage to large water mains. A large force of army personnel, mostly men of the Pioneer Corps, were immediately set to work by the regional authorities to repair the banks of the river; in the meantime, the fire service resources of the London region were mobilised to provide a relay to by-pass water across the breach. By this means, the total quantity of water being delivered into London was brought up to 20,000,000 gallons daily as against the normal volume of 46,000,000 gallons. Twelve pumps and 72 men were continuously engaged for more than three days, pumping water through 14 miles of hose laid by 12 hose lorries. By their efforts, the very serious threat to public safety and morale in London, posed by the possibility of a total lack of water was averted. By the evening of 19 October 1940, repair work was sufficiently in hand for the flow of water to be restored to its normal channel and all fire appliances and equipment were withdrawn.

A major fire broke out in the Oxford Circus area on the night of 17 October after an intense incendiary attack. Several large department stores were alight on all floors and water from street hydrants was scarce, even in this part of Central London criss-crossed with large-capacity water mains. The water available was insufficient to feed the fire pumps there, let alone the several hundred rapidly arriving at the scene. A hose relay was laid from Great Portland Street to the large lake in Regent's Park, a distance of about three-quarters of a mile. This was done by a hose-laying lorry and its attendant heavy pump unit capable of lifting the huge quantities of water from the relay source. The lengthy relay took about half an hour and was laid at somewhat more than the regulation twelve miles per hour! Once it was completed, the suction hose of the heavy pump unit was dropped into the lake and pumping began, but owing to the considerable frictional resistance in the long hose line, the heavy pump, although able to deliver 1,500gpm, needed several pumps interposed at intervals along the relay to boost the supply. All this activity consumed valuable time before the Regent's Park water started to arrive at Oxford Circus. By then it seemed that a large part of Oxford Street towards Tottenham Court

Road was ablaze, but once the reliable water supplies were available firemen were able to begin to contain and surround the fires. All were under control by dawn, although by this time John Lewis's store was a hollow charred shell.

The mornings after such raids usually provided a good deal of localised traffic congestion, as buses and other vehicles tried to manoeuvre past the assembled pumps still working at the kerbside and over the cobwebs of hose lines running in all directions.

In Cavendish Square, on the morning after the Oxford Street fires, Auxiliary Fireman Mac Young from Edgware Road Fire Station witnessed the early morning build-up of traffic and told a more junior and inexperienced colleague to do something about it; Mac did not want anything to scrape his much-cared-for trailer pump. Several minutes passed, by which time vehicles had ceased to wriggle past the fire service pumps. Apparently the well-intentioned young lad had redirected all the Wigmore Street traffic up a lengthy dead-end mews, buses and all. However, the honour of the AFS was restored when an attractive lone girl driving an Austin Seven seemed completely stranded by a large knot of charged hose lines. As if from nowhere, four burly firemen appeared and with one on each corner, bodily lifted the car and its occupant over the hose and set them down some yards away, clear of all the obstructions. Each fireman was seen to doff his helmet at the blushing young woman as she drove off hurriedly in the direction of Regent Street.

Then, on 3 November, for the very first night since the beginning of September, no Luftwaffe bombers appeared over London. It was a night of blissful peace for the duty watch of the LFS, except for several small localised fires caused by the odd cigarette-end or other domestic carelessness. Through September and October, the LFS had almost been able to set their watches by the first air-raid alert of each evening, such was the regularity and punctuality of the German bombing and now, quite suddenly, nothing.

The Relentless Raids

As Londoners slept undisturbed on this first sweet night of respite the red LFB appliances, trailer pumps, heavy units, hose lorries and their respective crews, waited. In the watch-rooms of fire stations across London the telephones and fire-alarm panels remained strangely silent and the AFS girls were able to sip their tea undisturbed. No one yet dared hope that this was the end of London's ordeal by fire. The ordeal had lasted for fifty-seven consecutive nights, during which the capital had suffered some of the wildest events in its history.

6

Coventry, Convoys, and the City Raid

The brief respite afforded London by the Luftwaffe from early November 1940 onwards did not allow the battle-weary fire-fighters much of a rest and recovery period, for within days Goering had turned his attacks on provincial cities. Coventry suffered a particularly heavy raid of incendiaries and high explosives on 14 November, and this aerial pounding lasted for eleven hours and killed more than 500 civilians. Coventry Fire Brigade was able to contain the serious situation for about four hours before it became clear that its efforts would be insufficient to prevent a fire storm obliterating the city; the centre, including the historic cathedral, was one large mass of flame. Chaos reigned as fire-fighting reinforcements were urgently called for from other regions. But as pumps and men arrived from neighbouring brigades there was little co-ordination of effort, little water for fire-fighting and petrol for the pumps was scarce. Telephone communications had all but failed throughout the city.

Fifty men from the LFS were sent in buses to Coventry on the day following the raid, but when they arrived in the devastated city they were hard put to find pumps to use. The London men found Coventry in a totally dazed state after its traumatic exposure to the German bombers and they must have been deeply frustrated by the official decision, taken at senior regional level, to transport them there minus their pumps. Several days later, London was asked to provide a small number of appliances for Coventry. Auxiliary Fireman

Trevor Hughes was a crew member on this first convoy from London which left for the Midland city on 19 November:

It was a dull November day when we joined the rest of the convoy at our Superintendent Station. I telegraphed home, then climbed on to the heavy unit, and at ten o'clock we were on our way.

The convoy consisted of two hose laying lorries, each carrying 6,000ft of hose, four heavy pumping units, a utility lorry and two dispatch riders on motor cycles. As each heavy unit carried a crew of ten men instead of the usual six or seven, some of us had to travel standing in the open, and I preferred to ride that way.

It is apparent that most of the fires had burned themselves out by this time, for the London convoy received orders to pause overnight in Rugby before pressing on for Coventry next morning.

The direct journey from Rugby to Coventry was not more than about fourteen miles; we did not know, then, that the main road was blocked, and that, at the first cross-roads, the convoy leader had been instructed to make a wide detour. I imagined we were already near Coventry when we ran into a heavy storm. The roads were flooding, water swept our deck, and the other appliances vanished behind impenetrable screens of rain.

Sensibly, the rest of the men took what little cover was available; the rain was beating coldly, violently, against me, so that I had sometimes to turn my head aside for breath. The water forced its way beneath the storm collar of my water-proof and ran icily down my chest; but heart and eyes were straining always ahead as I waited for the first glimpse of Coventry. As Damascus to T. E. Lawrence, so Coventry was significant to me as the first stepping stone towards a new world. How hungrily, I realized, had Lawrence waited, during that last march, for the first glimpse of Damascus.

The storm ended as suddenly as it began. Hazily, at first, then clearly, we saw the three distant spires of Coventry. We passed a burnt out farmhouse, then a street of shattered houses, signs of damage multiplying quickly until we turned into the Coventry station square. At the roadside a long queue of people moved slowly towards a line of canteen vans. On the farther side were several fire service trailer pumps, blackened, burnt out, sometimes twisted almost beyond recognition by blast or impact. While we were waiting for instructions a local Service man told us something of the raids.

'How did your men get on?' we asked. He shrugged his shoulders.

'Most of them got it in the head or chest. You see, they never went down to the bombs. There were thirteen men round one pump . . .'

We drove on past a tramcar which stood, battered and abandoned, on a wide-swept corner. Then, at converging roads, we found ourselves looking down into the shattered heart of Coventry. Nothing had been spared, nothing survived the fury, the fire and murder, which had engulfed those streets.

We looked down into a disintegrated city, into mighty and unending mounds of broken brick and glass, and writhing, black shapes of ironwork and wood; down long depressions in the debris where had been prosperous streets; down into a structureless abyss of chaos and destruction, where lay the beneficence, the nothingness and the stillness, of overwhelming death; down into acres of sprawling desolation and an unforgettable dead-moon waste; down into the dismal, cold contortion of a Dantesque place, into an unparalleled world of sorrow and confusion, of ruin incomprehensible, complete.

Nothing could be done. We were helpless before such things, and before those who had endured the three searing nights. We saw them drifting past, not recognizing friends, not talking amongst themselves, or recounting their experiences, their escapes, but walking slowly, silently, with mechanical, aimless steps and unseeing eyes; lost ghosts moving along the well remembered shadows of a fallen city. Their eyes were tired and bewildered, their minds numbed to the knowledge of bereavement, and overwrought by pain, and shock, and horror unimaginable. Some stopped and looked around like men who dreamed. But none gave any sign of despair; nor did they smile any more.

In every London raid the courage of the people had inspired us. We had seen the light of faith and humour shining unwaveringly in unexpected places, a kindling torch carried swiftly from man to man through desperate nights of historic darkness.

. . . We were sent on to a narrow street where fire still burned under the wreckage of a printing works. We went down a hoist-shaft and through a wide passage into the basement, an occasional leap of flame showing us a large room where scattered heaps of debris smouldered on a concrete floor. Shadows danced about the dark outlines of twisted metal, the threatening glow from the floor rising and falling rhythmatically—what gruesome fantasies would Poe have weaved about them. The air was heavy, and the heat so intense that we had to shield our faces with our arms. It was decided that the men should work in relays of two and be relieved at ten minute intervals until the heat could be dispersed.

Our water supply was from a canvas dam at a distant crossroads, and some of us found our way to it by following the line of hose. Canteen vans were everywhere. At many street corners motor water tanks were supplying domestic needs. A queue of dejected people stood outside the Public Assistance Office. There was some talk of German bombing methods, and of our own inadequate defences. One woman was describing how she and her family had spent three nights in a cupboard under the stairs. 'On the third night,' she said, 'the whole house came down on top of us. We tried to open the door, but it was jammed. We were hungry when they dug us out. Yes,' she added slowly, 'God is good.' Then, startling in its eagerness, 'You haven't got a cigarette to spare, have you?'

In the street near the dam smoke was rising from the shells of two houses. Roofs and floors had fallen into the basements, yet the entrance porch of the first house was intact, its tiled floor clean although flames seemed to emanate from the doorstep itself. We hacked some tiles away, and ran out a line of hose, but, after several attempts, we found it impossible to obtain enough water pressure.

A girl from a house nearby told us that six tons of coal and some gallons of olive oil had been burning in the cellar for three days. 'Our air-raid shelter is flooded with water,' she said. 'Couldn't you use that?' But we had no pump to lift it.

At the next house we found a damaged bucket and an outside tank full of water. I stood on a crumbling slope below the hall, and, as the men handed me the water, threw it through a gap in the debris. But before it reached the coal the heat converted it to steam which blew back into my face. There were tiny explosions underfoot. The air was hot and sulphurous, and I could breathe only by swinging away from the thick white smoke.

I hoped to visit the cathedral, but spent some time at a hose lorry helping to re-stow the wet hose. Then the OC told me he was ready to start back and that I could see the cathedral in the morning. I could not explain how much I wanted to see it that night.

The London convoy stopped overnight again at Rugby and whilst they were there another raid occurred over the battered city they had just left. On the journey back to the capital, a rear tyre of one of the pumps burst and the appliance almost went into a hedge. Hughes recalled:

> We explored the little hamlet while a new tyre was being fitted. An old man told us proudly how the aeroplanes flew low to frighten them; one had even dropped some incendiary bombs in the Long Meadow. At least, I think he meant incendiary bombs.

When the London contingent finally returned to their own stations after dark, they found a quiet evening in progress, with most pumps in.

CONVOYS

The fire-fighting lesson at Coventry had been learnt, for when the Luftwaffe attacked Birmingham in some force on 23 November, an LFS convoy of fifteen pumps and two water units and crews were dispatched northwards within hours of the raid to assist the local forces.

During this period, the Luftwaffe switched the pattern of the raids between London and the ports, and when Southampton was the target for a big raid in the last week of November, a large London contingent was again sent out; by 2 December this totalled 400 officers, men and women, 20 pumps, 4 water units, 4 canteen vans (manned by AFS women) and 4 lorries.

LFB Chief Superintendent Arthur Sullivan, had been one of the experienced officers seconded to the Home Office along with Commander Firebrace in 1939, in order to prepare a war footing for London's fire defence. Sullivan was retained to join Firebrace's staff at regional HQ when war broke out and had, up to this time, little chance to get involved in the 'front line'. However, when Southampton's fire-fighting looked near to collapse after the first major raid, Sullivan was sent to assess the situation. On 1 December he found many fires still burning fiercely and a motley collection of appliances from other brigades in the city, but few being used to advantage. Southampton's chief fire officer was, in Sullivan's own words, 'mentally and physically exhausted'. Exercising the powers of Home Secretary, Sullivan sent many local officers off duty for a rest, organised the city into six sectors and put each in the charge of an outside senior fire officer. By the time the King and Queen visited Southampton later that week, all the fires were out but there were huge gaps in rows of buildings everywhere.

Frank Reader was an auxiliary who manned a pump from Shoreditch which went to Southampton. Coming on duty at their Daniel Street sub-station, his crew was detailed to rendezvous with other London appliances on the Great West Road at Brentford to receive further orders. At this stage, no one seemed to know where they were going. Frank and his crew spent three days and nights fire-fighting in the city and recalled that the grey London appliances looked very untidy—dented, scratched and generally battered contrasted with some of the rural pumps that had also gone to help with the port fires. One machine from Oxfordshire even sported brightly polished chrome delivery controls, wheel rims and other parts: it looked as if it had never been used in anger. It was a far cry from the London blitz.

Recently Reader vividly remembered one Southampton night that he spent perched 40ft up on an iron staircase working a hissing and writhing water jet, looking down into a gaping void which had been the Union Cold Storage Building near the docks. He recalled the powerful aroma of roasting meat continually rising up and enveloping him as thousands of tons of carcases cooked below, tempting his ravenous appetite. The sudden staccato sound of anti-aircraft fire made him jump and the whole rickety staircase shook under his weight. But Reader was remote from his pump operator and could not abandon his high-pressure jet to shelter from his exposed position. Few nozzles used by the AFS had a shut-off valve and in order to close down a fire-fighting jet a fireman had to retrace the hose line back to the supplying pump, then close down the appropriate delivery valve. With dozens of hoses littering the streets, often intertwining, this could be a difficult and frustrating task. Fortunately, the 'raider' on that occasion turned out to be a German reconnaissance aircraft surveying Southampton's damage and the firemen were left to get on with their wearying tasks.

Back in London, virtually all the units of the LFS were in action again on the night of 8 December, when over 400 enemy aircraft dropped 3,188 incendiary loads over a wide area of the capital. By morning, over 2,000 fires had been successfully dealt with.

Whilst the approach of Christmas saw another short lull in the enemy action over London, an air-raid over the Manchester area caused fires that, like those at Coventry and Southampton, put fire-fighters under extreme and immediate pressure. Again, the London region was asked to mobilise some urgent assistance and on 23 December, 300 officers, men and women, with a convoy of 40 pumps, 6 canteen vans and 7 lorries loaded down with hose, left for Manchester. Such reinforcements were drawn from fire stations in a wide area of the region in order not to deplete London's fire cover too drastically. Thus successive pumps in the northbound convoy could be drawn from different districts—West Norwood, North Kensington, Stoke Newington and Eltham, for example.

The two days of Christmas 1940 were not disturbed by the drone of enemy aircraft and apart from a few normal call-outs to domestic fires, most of London's fire stations were quiet.

An LFB officer braves the intense heat and falling debris to check the spreading fire situation. Note the narrow gap between buildings on either side. Amen Court, City of London, close by St Paul's Cathedral. 29 December 1940 (*Daily Mirror*)

The City of London burns – a view taken from the dome of St Paul's looking towards Cheapside. 29 December 1940 (*Daily Mirror*)

A burnt-out tramcar stands abandoned. Victoria Embankment, SW1. 29 December 1940 (*Daily Mirror*)

It was perhaps a chance for the regular and AFS crews on duty to relax their guard a little and get some much-needed rest. More resourceful stations were able to provide some minimal festive fare and a few decorations, and by now most sub-stations could be made warm and cosy. During the autumn of 1940 a few had even discovered that the alloy cases of un-damaged German incendiaries, when chopped into small pieces, made excellent fast burning fuel for the mess room fires. Explaining away the eventual disintegration of the fire grates took some doing.

Christmas was to be short-lived. During the early evening of 27 December the sirens sounded a red alert and within minutes of the wailing tones ceasing, the first bombs crashed down over London. However, even with the number of men and pumps committed to Manchester, the LFS was able to cope with more than 1,000 fires that evening, all of which were under control by dawn.

THE CITY RAID

Two days later came one of London's most savage, concen-trated incendiary bomb attacks of the war. The area of the historic City of London contained half a square mile known to the LFS as 'the danger zone'. This was the tightly packed group of warehouses, workshops, offices and churches around Wood Street, St Martin's-le-Grand and St Paul's Cathedral. Most narrow alleyways and passages that ran between the buildings were glazed over and all the warehouses had stocks of flammable materials. The buildings themselves were old and mostly built of wood.

The tragedy of that night is that much of the subsequent damage could have been avoided if the occupiers of the premises had provided some basic provision for fire watchers to deal with incendiaries, just as many ARP wardens, police-men and householders were progressively and more confidently doing. But on that fateful night there were few such fire watchers, as on a Sunday hardly any people were in this district for not many actually lived in what was primarily a business quarter of London. Most buildings were double padlocked; even after four months of the blitz it seemed that few commercial companies had learned the value of an early attack on an incipient fire.

The raiding force, which was a relatively small one of 130 aircraft, appeared over the City soon after 6pm and began systematic incendiary bombing of this vulnerable part of London. Within minutes, fires were burning in roofs in Cheapside, Queen Victoria Street and near to the Guildhall in Gresham Street. The fires rapidly grew and leapt from roof to roof before the first LFS appliances came clanging into the area from Cannon Street, Redcross Street and White-friars. The first fire-fighters on the scene could see that they had a major battle ahead. A serious fire situation was simul-taneously developing across the river at Southwark, where a riverside warehouse was alight from incendiaries which had missed their City targets.

Although it was mainly a fire raid, the inevitable few high explosives crashed down amid the clattering of the incen-diaries and were sufficient not only to damage most of the smaller water mains in the City streets all around the fires, but to break twelve large trunk water mains which ran right through the City square mile itself. The emergency supply laid from the Thames northwards through the area was also made useless by bombing before the raid was even an hour old. Pump after pump failed as its water supply dried up and crews of firemen on all sides of the fire zone gradually lost their water armament and were forced to retreat.

Within half an hour messages were received that fires in the vicinity of St Paul's Cathedral were spreading and that further assistance was required. A number of messages also reported serious fires elsewhere in the City and in the Mino-ries, Southwark and Dockhead areas. An hour after the night's activities had begun it was reported that a fire situation in

Golden Lane, in the northern portion of the City, was developing and further urgent assistance was required. In view of the number of fires in the London County Council area at this time, the regional scheme was again called into operation.

By 8pm approximately, 300 pumps had been called for in the City and central districts. It was also reported that fires in Queen Victoria Street were spreading—there was a severe shortage of water in this area—and that a fire in St Martin's-le-Grand was assuming serious proportions. Shortly afterwards fires in the Minories were out of hand owing to a lack of water and those in Gresham Street were still spreading.

From that time on, the three main fire areas (City, Minories and Southwark) assumed alarming proportions and urgent messages for help were being taken to the district control centres by dispatch rider. Every available pump was now being mobilised irrespective of the need for local cover. The City area was protected by four LFB fire stations and a number of AFS sub-stations. One LFB station had already suffered damage and Redcross Street sub-district station—the control point for the entire area in the early stages—now found itself close to the advancing flames. The City fire-control function was therefore transferred to Cannon Street Fire Station, but this building too was soon threatened, and control was finally established at Whitefriars Street Fire Station off Fleet Street. Nine separate control points staffed by senior officers at various places on the outer fringe of the fire zone were linked to Whitefriars Street, although it was some time before the deluge of requests for more men and machines was co-ordinated.

St Paul's was one of the few buildings in the area which had any effective fire watchers. When the first incendiaries had started to fall on the roofs of the lower levels of the cathedral, waiting vergers and choirboys were ready with buckets of sand and water to deal with the fiery devices. One incendiary lodged itself high up on the dome of St Paul's, impossibly

125

out of reach of both the stirrup pumps of the cathedral fire party and the more powerful jets of the LFS. At the time neither had a great deal of water, but fortunately the threatening bomb suddenly fell backwards into the stone gallery and was dealt with quickly at close quarters. For the moment, St Paul's had been saved, although in the streets all around Wren's masterpiece a fire storm was growing. Thousands of huge burning fragments were whipped up into the sky where they swirled like clouds of angry orange locusts in the light of the reflected flames.

The spread of fire was phenomenal, encouraged by a strong wind. Auxiliary Fireman Mac Young had gone to Cheapside with a trailer pump from his Paddington sub-station at about 6pm. He started pumping with what limited water was available at the Bank of England end of Cheapside. His hose line leading away from the trailer pump was feeding a jet further up, near St Paul's. To Mac Young, it seemed that most of the worst fires were up that end of Cheapside. Within an hour of his crew's arrival the fires had insidiously worked their way along the roofs of Cheapside and were now almost directly over his head. Mac Young can remember today the rigid LFB discipline even in the face of such potential disaster. A superintendent suddenly appeared and caught him smoking. Worse still, Young had a single tunic button undone and his belt and axe worn far from the correct central position. Fortunately for the AFS man a nearby length of hose suddenly burst and spewed a fountain of valuable water into the gutter, and the worst of the LFB officer's invective was spared as they both struggled to shut down the damaged hose. This was the same superintendent who had previously shown his own individual style of defiance to the Luftwaffe by forsaking his steel helmet for a museum-piece Victorian brass helmet, and by going from fire to fire wearing white gloves.

Another auxiliary recalled how he had been driving an officer on that evening and acted as a messenger:

There was fire in every direction. The City was turned into an enormous, loosely-stacked furnace—belching black smoke. The sky above was red with the glow, and the smoke as it drifted upwards was reddened on its underside, but deep black when seen against the sky. Anywhere near the fire itself the heat and light combined to give an illusion of unreality.

Gradually the black smoke was turned to steam as the thousands of tons of water poured onto the fire. White ash fell everywhere—on the roads, on the car windscreen, on the men. Our eyes smarted. Some of the men I spoke to could hardly see at all.

The heat blistered the car paint. It blistered the men's faces. It blistered the pumps. I would go round a corner with Adams and meet suddenly with a wall of fire. Quite involuntarily we would both cover our faces with our arms. It hurt your eyes, hurt your nose. My chin was quite badly burnt and it blistered. As the roofs went in, so the sparks belched from the windows, as if blown by giant bellows. Then the shells of the buildings made well-ventilated, giant chimneys, and the rubble roared on into the ashes.

A large number of the reinforcing pumps and crews were alerted to bring additional water to the fire area but the Luftwaffe had chosen their night well. At the height of the raid the Thames was at a very low ebb, and getting to what water there was meant a waist-deep wallow through thick mud by firemen, as they attempted to connect lines of hose to the waiting fireboats far out in the tideway. Trailer pumps were manhandled down stone steps on to the edges of the mud and lowered on lines into the soft edges of the river from London, Southwark and Blackfriars Bridges, in repeated valiant efforts to get the huge quantities of sorely needed water from the Thames. In the meantime the fires in the City burnt on, consuming fresh buildings by the minute.

The Wren churches suffered. St Bride and Wren's own favourite, St James, were early casualties, their tinder-dry roof beams quickly weakening and collapsing into the fiery interiors. Virtually powerless to stop the flames because of an almost total lack of water, a Cockney fireman was heard to remark: 'Bleeding lot o' wood that bloke Wren used, didn' 'ee?'

With over 300 pumps at work in the City, there came a report at about 9pm that the imminent collapse of the steeple of St Lawrence Jewry was threatening the Guildhall, but only a few pumps could be spared to investigate. For about half an hour a sporadic fall of high-explosive bombs took place right across the City fire zone, and by 9.45pm the first messages to the control centre from the historic timbered building stated that the main turret of the Guildhall was alight and that more assistance was urgently required. Another large fire zone was developing in the Minories district near the Tower of London as a result of a small but concentrated incendiary attack. Around the Guildhall a quarter of a square mile area of unabating fire had developed. This was caused by an initial lack of pumps and men, and the fire controls found it hard to split and deploy reinforcements as they became available.

By 10pm only thirty pumps remained in fire stations in reserve, these being scattered around the wide ring of outer London to provide some basic fire cover for the capital. A total of 1,700 were now at work in the City or the Minories or Southwark; this was almost as many fire appliances as were available for the entire United Kingdom before the war. Home Office Control were asked to provide 300 additional pumps from outer regions for the London area, and for the first time a number of bulk water carriers were ordered into the City from outer rural areas. By this time the huge fires in the City, right in the heart of London, could be seen over thirty miles away, and the pumps hurrying in from all directions needed little guidance to their destination. The sky around St Paul's was coloured deep orange and a scarlet glow reflected the immense dome of the cathedral. Every street, alleyway and footpath was littered with hose lines, some limp and flaccid, others pulsating with water passing through. On every street corner were AFS heavy pumping units, trailer pumps and regular LFB machines. Many pumps were being run at full throttle to maintain pressure on the branches (nozzles) and their exhausts glowed red. Crews of firemen ran to and fro, shouting to each other and trying to get water on to some nearby inferno. Water from those jets at work was turned black by the fires and eventually ran back down stairs or streamed off roofs, finally to cascade down gutters in constant torrents. Eerily, all across the City of London, fell fine particles of white ash like some gentle benign snowstorm.

This was a night when the Luftwaffe clearly intended to raze the central core of London. Women members of the AFS played a stoic role in the defence of the City. Into the danger zone of burning and collapsing buildings they went with their petrol carriers, each braving the cascading sparks to ferry a load of cans of highly flammable fuel to replenish the hundreds of roaring pumps. The AFS girls also crewed the canteen vans, parked as safely from fire-fighting operations as they could be, brewing gallons of tea. Yet few firemen could be spared to take refreshment before midnight and many worked on into the early hours without respite from the flames, heat, smoke and their own sodden uniforms. Auxiliary firewomen also drove the senior officers in staff cars in the fire zones and waited whilst their officers assessed the local situation, checked on spreading fire and generally made an urgent appreciation of the vicinity.

These women drivers of petrol carriers, canteen vans and staff cars, were the only females to be seen in the City area that night. Auxiliary Firewoman Peggy Joseph recalled an amusing incident that took place around midnight. She was driving an LFB superintendent and since the raid started had steered the staff car over lines of snaking hose and around heaps of steaming rubble strewn across the streets. Eventually she arrived in Redcross Street and the superintendent had hurried off into the smoky glow having told Peggy to wait. She, however, felt the urgent need to relieve a call of nature, but where? Much of the street was as bright as day with the flickering light from the many fires. The occasional bomb still came shrieking down to explode close by and every few yards there seemed to be firemen. The sound of water gushing along gutters and from a burst length of hose nearby did nothing to help Peggy's predicament. She was forced into action. Taking refuge behind a partially blown-out building frontage, she decided that her need was greater than all other considerations. By the time the superintendent returned some minutes later, Peggy was indeed able to report that she was still OK before they moved on to another sector of the fire.

Shortly after this, the situation in the Redcross Street area became grave. Fire, collapsing buildings and debris were clearly beginning to isolate a number of streets. Fifteen pumps and their crews hard at work in nearby Whitecross Street found themselves almost cut off by fire. Several firemen working a branch were forced to turn their water onto their own fire pump as it burst into flame from the tremendous radiated heat coming off the burning premises all along the street. Several minutes passed before the senior officer was forced to order the evacuation of all personnel in the area. This included a number of AFS girls still manning telephones in Redcross Street Fire Station. Every pump was abandoned where it was parked. One by one, the jets were rapidly shut down to enable the men closest to the fires to pull back. Soon a stream of firemen and women made their way between the ruins of St Giles, Cripplegate, which had been badly damaged in an earlier raid, and a large warehouse that was well alight. They dropped down into an empty air-raid shelter which led out on to the underground railway tracks of the Metropolitan line. Gingerly following these, the escaping party passed under the flames above to arrive eventually at Smithfield Goods Depot and relative safety. Where they stood only minutes before, whole streets had joined together in a raging mass of continuous flame.

'ALL CLEAR'—BUT NOT FOR FIREMEN

Yet to the astonishment of the fire-fighters and Civil Defence workers, the 'all clear' suddenly sounded at 9.45pm. This was an unusually early hour for the respite to have come, although by this time much damage had been caused. Eight of Wren's churches and many livery halls, offices and warehouses had burnt like torches. The Tower of London and the Law Courts had been hit and even when the 'all clear' came, many City fires were burning out of control. To the further surprise of the fire-fighters below, the Luftwaffe failed to press home the attack. Indeed, had the bombing been sustained or had a second raid taken place around midnight, the eventual outcome could well have been the destruction of the City of London.

Even so, around 10.30pm the Guildhall roof had fallen inwards sending up a shower of fiery fragments into the night sky as if guided by some invisible chimney. But all was not despair. As the night wore on, the Thames tide slowly turned and its level began to rise gradually. Then it became a little easier for the waiting pump crews to lower their suction hose into the water, although many bogged-down trailer pumps that had been laboriously dragged out into the muddy edges of the river earlier in the evening had to be abandoned as the water rose. Existing hose relays from the fireboats were added to as the fire-fighting craft were able to come closer alongside the various piers and jetties along the northern banks close under St Paul's. Soon more water was pouring from the Thames along the maze of hose to the waiting pumps and firemen. From 3am, with the river in full flood, the fire-fighters began to get the flames under control for the first time since the raid began. The lesser outbreaks at the Minories and in Southwark were already under control, but still required hundreds of men and machines.

Perhaps for the first time in the entire London blitz, there was a sense of how near to defeat the LFS had come on this single night. Auxiliary Fireman Philip Henderson clearly highlighted this feeling:

> We stand at the end of an avenue of fire, curiously detached and isolated before a monstrous conflagration that leaps and towers above us into its own livid day. The heat is so intense that we dry our soaked neckcloths on top of our tin hats.
>
> There is nothing we can do. Two or three radial branches are already pouring solid arcs of water into the heart of the fire and a water tower is attacking it from a side street. Moreover the outside brigades are beginning to come in. Let them have a dose. We've had our basinful. Somebody says there is a canteen van just round the corner.
>
> With hands and faces blackened as miners, we line up for our mugs of cocoa. A tin of biscuits is passed round; each man dives in and grabs a handful, and for every mug returned there is a slab of chocolate.
>
> In silence we sit on the kerb, on the steps of offices and shops. Reaching for a smoke, I find that all my cigarettes have been reduced to a damp yellow pulp.
>
> Morning is already breaking. In the first grey light the charred devastation looks indescribably dreary. It seems to objectify our sick weariness and all the nausea of war.
>
> 'I suppose this is what the poor bastards over there get too,' somebody remarks.
>
> Returning to the station we find that seven of our men are missing. Later we hear that four of them are so badly burned as to be hardly recognizable. Suddenly, as they turned a corner in the City, the whole of Chiswell Street was ablaze. Jumping from the tender they tried to run for it: they ran into a collapsing wall of fire, scalded and blinded by flame. They fainted while fighting their way out and were picked up later, it seems, by soldiers on leave who had come to lend a hand.
>
> The next morning I saw the wife of one of them sitting with a white blank face in the station officer's room. We tried not to notice her as we went on with our daily routine of sweeping and cleaning.

Of 1,500 fires logged in the London region on that night, all but 28 were in the square mile of the City of London. Damping-down operations lasted well into the next night and included the recovery of fifteen burnt-out pumps abandoned in White-cross Street.

During the fire-fighting operations on 29–30 December, 14 firemen were killed and over 250 men and women seriously injured. Among 17 awards for gallantry given to members of the LFS after this raid, 4 were awarded to auxiliary firewomen, mostly for their courage whilst driving essential vehicles in the face of falling bombs.

This night in December underlined the need for occupiers to maintain a constant vigil on their premises. Amid the smouldering and gutted buildings which faced the City workers that morning, stood the proud and relatively un-scathed outline of St Paul's; not only was its survival a power-ful symbol, but it was a clear indication of the value of fire watchers. Apparently Winston Churchill thought so too. At a cabinet meeting later that day, Monday, 30 December, the prime minister ordered that such an incendiary raid should never again be unleashed on unguarded buildings. A Fire Precautions Order was hurried through parliament, requiring local authorities and government departments to make ar-rangements for 'detecting and combating fires' in prescribed business and industrial areas. Males between the ages of sixteen and sixty were obliged to register as part-time fire watchers and had to perform such duties for up to forty-eight hours a month.

The raids on the London region from September to Decem-ber killed almost 13,000 civilians, with a further 20,000 seriously wounded. An estimated 36,000 high-explosive bombs (excluding incendiaries) were dropped during this time, a bomb weight of 6,600 tons. Goering boasted that in the raid of 29 December the Luftwaffe had dropped 100,000 incendiaries.

Thus ended 1940, a year which had seen a complete turn-around in the fortunes of the London firemen and women. They had experienced the inactivity of the early months through to the hectic nightly battering of September and

October, and had suddenly found that the public considered the AFS to be something more than 'column dodgers' after all. But as the new year arrived most personnel in the LFS were growing weary. How much longer would these raids last? The City fire raid of 29 December had very nearly broken the resolve and the resources of London's fire-fighters and there was no indication that 1941 would bring any improvement for those who had to stand their ground and face what came.

7
Recovery and Breathing Space

The coming of the new year marked a continued easing off of the regular heavy night raids over London and it certainly appeared that the Luftwaffe had no enduring long-term bombing strategy. During the first month of 1941 there were only four nights, 9, 11, 12 and 29 January, when the bombers made their familiar way over London, dropping the incendiaries and high explosives upon targets ranging from Dockland in the east to Fulham in the west. However, during this month there were heavy raids on Portsmouth and Bristol, where severe damage was inflicted. Firemen from the London region formed hastily convened convoys to both these centres. For Portsmouth, a force which included 101 pumps, 6 water and 30 dam units, 3 petrol tank waggons, 7 canteen vans and 32 dispatch riders, was sent late on the evening of 10 January. This force was augmented by 200 LFS officers and men dispatched to the port by train to relieve Portsmouth's own firemen.

The intense raid over London on the night of 11 January had looked like developing into a very major affair; with the incessant bombing only two hours old, London Regional Control was asking the Home Office Control Centre for the urgent release of the LFS appliances in Portsmouth. Only a few of the pumps could be spared and by the time these arrived back in the capital, the night's fires had already been beaten into submission.

Although the fire service convoys may have been a useful expediency in 1940, the deployment of LFS contingents to various provincial cities during early 1941 caused increasingly frequent difficulties. Often, the size of the arriving London contingent was far greater than the total number of men of the fire brigade they were reinforcing. The London convoys always consisted of a mixture of LFB and AFS officers and men, and were commanded by a senior ranking officer, thus creating a very experienced team. Attempts by the London officers to take charge of a fire area in a provincial town or city were frequently resented and their orders were, in some cases, countermanded by junior members of the local force. There were examples of water relays being set up by London men and then diverted by local crews to less important fires. Friction between the London officers and men and their counterparts began to be open. Yet the Home Office, which had the ultimate responsibility for ordering the London reinforcements in the first place, chose to do little to ease the situation. During the winter of 1941 the Home Office did issue a memorandum urging all local authorities to plan more carefully for such contingencies including, amongst other things, rendezvous and reporting points for the incoming fire-fighters. Sadly, this memorandum seems to have been largely ignored.

February 1941 was a memorable month for the LFS. No major raids occurred in any part of London. It was a month of continued poor weather, with low cloud and many nights of rain, mist and fog. In addition to the difficult flying conditions, a growing number of anti-aircraft gun and searchlight positions were sprouting up around London and the suburbs and these were becoming more effective at harassing enemy fliers.

It was also a month of consolidation for the LFS. The lull gave opportunities for men to be released from front-line duties to attend courses on breathing apparatus and turntable-ladder operation and for some men to transfer to the river section. Crews at stations were able to listen uninterrupted to technical lectures, sort out missing equipment and organise repairs to damaged fire-fighting gear. The large central workshop behind the Lambeth HQ of the LFS had continued to function throughout the blitz. It was capable of dealing with the heaviest appliances and coped with all ladder, pump and hose repairs as well as housing large stores of hundreds of ancillary items.

Although the Luftwaffe concentrated its activities on centres as distant as Swansea, Merseyside, Bristol and Hull in the first weeks of March, London did receive two consecutive nights' raiding on 8 and 9 March, and another heavy attack on 19 March. The latter raid took the usual form of the raids of the previous autumn—the red alert sounded at 6.30pm and bombing started over a wide area of London shortly after. On this night, 479 bombers dropped over 3,000 baskets of incendiaries, together with the familiar 'mix' of high explosives. By dawn, 750 Londoners had been killed, but all the night's 1,880 fires were under control, though some were still burning. A woman stood surveying the remains of her burnt-out home in the East End the morning after this raid; an LFS officer asked her 'Where's your husband, love?' 'In Libya, the bloody coward!' was the immediate retort.

After the 19 March raid, London was spared another major attack for almost four weeks. This period saw the issue to stations of the first purpose-built vehicles for towing the trailer pumps. Whilst still performing yeoman service, the London taxis pressed into use in 1939 were hardly a long-term answer for the LFS: the cabs had taken a tremendous hammering over the previous six months. Much hose and equipment was piled into the rear of the cabs leaving little room for the crew members. Hiring arrangements for the cabs were also proving a financial drain on LFS resources and more suitable replacements were urgently needed. The new vehicles were Austin two-ton vans with seats in the rear for the men and locker space for hose and small gear, with an extension ladder on the roof.

The Home Office also made available much larger quantities of lengths of 6in diameter steel piping which allowed semipermanent emergency water mains to be laid along the surface of streets in high-risk areas. The pipe-lengths came with various couplings and adaptors, tee-pieces and elbow-joints designed to carry a pipeline around street fittings. Given a crew of firemen well used to the laying and joining-up procedure, the pipelines could be laid at the rate of about a mile an hour. These surface-laid water mains were still susceptible to direct hits but had the great advantage of being able to absorb much of the shock of high explosives falling nearby, unlike the conventional underground mains which could crack and rupture unseen beneath the ground: the steel pipelines merely bounced or sprang a few small leaks at the joints. Unfortunately, nowhere near enough pipeline was available in London at this time and when, in the later months of 1941, more began to arrive, it was too late to be of any use; the worst of the major fire raids were over by then.

Other actions helped the fire service to strengthen the organisation and its capability. In early 1940, the age reservation for AFS firemen had been put at thirty and men between that age and fifty had been allowed to join the AFS instead of military service, but few did so. The loss of personnel to the service through death and injury was considerable and the general intention at Home Office level was to increase the numbers of the AFS to enable the maximum number of pumps to be manned at all times. Accordingly, the National Service Act of April 1941 gave the authorities power to conscript men into the fire service. Over the remaining years of the war, 20,000 firemen were drafted directly into fire-fighting forces nationally.

The Bristol region was again reinforced by a London convoy sent to Avonmouth Docks on 30 March. This convoy took with it a large quantity of London foam-making equipment and foam-producing compound to supplement local resources. This was made necessary by a very large petrol and oil fire in the tanks of the Avonmouth complex, caused by a sharp incendiary attack.

View looking along Whitecross Street, EC, the morning after the intense City raid. The remains of burnt-out and bombed fire pumps litter the roadway. From this street, a number of firemen were forced to abandon their equipment and retreat to safety. 30 December 1940 (*LFB*)

Damage to historic buildings continued throughout the air raids of 1940–41. The charred roof timbers of the Guildhall Banqueting Hall have fallen in some hours back and the carved figures bear silent witness to a battle lost the night before. The City raid – 30 December 1940 (*LFB*)

A 100 foot turntable ladder at work supplementing the work of crews in the street. Buildings on both sides of the narrow street are alight. Note firemen at head of ladder directing water jet. Stewart Street, Shoreditch, EC. 11 January 1941 (*Daily Mirror*)

APRIL RAIDS

Just when optimism was rising and it was hoped that the worst fires were past, twice in a single week came extremely severe and taxing raids over a wide area of the capital. The first of these raids, on 16 April, was notable for producing a greater number of fires than ever before in one single raid. At midnight, the London region's fire total stood at 2,300 separate incidents and of these, over 1,500 were in the London County Council area. Although no conflagrations were recorded, there were nearly 400 serious fires. All the available pumps were in use, emergency working was put into operation during the night, and to cover the depleted outer areas of London 120 pumps were loaned from other regions. The efforts of the London Fire Service brought the situation under control by early morning and it was not necessary to use the extra-regional forces which were returned to their home areas later in the day. Several important water mains were broken during the night but the water unit service was able to cope with all emergencies, despite the fact that the Thames tide was low at the pitch of the raid. Fire watchers dealt with thousands of incendiary bombs and contributed materially towards keeping down the large number of smaller fires. In the City, St Paul's had been hit again, this time by a 500lb bomb and a cluster of incendiaries, but the constant attention of the cathedral fire watchers paid off and all the fires were quickly stamped out.

A graphic account of some of that night's fury was re-counted by an LFB superintendent who, along with his AFS woman driver, had gone from one district to another:

On the evening of 16 April 1941, the sirens sounded early, and I stood by in fire kit in the District Control awaiting the receipt of calls. Shortly after the raid started, one was received from the BBC in Portland Place. I at once ordered my car and went on. On arrival the officer-in-charge reported to me that he had made it a ten pump fire. A very large bomb had devastated the rear of the main building of the BBC, also involving the annexe. About a dozen buildings were well alight, and the fire was spreading. I took over control, made it a thirty pump fire and requested two turntable ladders.

Upon the arrival of the Chief Superintendent I turned over to him, and, taking a party of men, I commenced a search in the rear part of the building, which had taken the full impact of the bomb and blast. Where once had stood a series of two, three and four storied buildings was now only a heap of rubble. During the progress of the fire, other small fires, caused by flying embers, broke out on surrounding roofs, and it was necessary to keep the turntable ladders constantly on the move in order to attack them.

During the course of operations, there was a sudden change in the direction of the wind, and I noticed the branchman at the top of one of the ladders suddenly become enveloped in flame. Instructions were immediately given for him to be brought down, and he was taken to my car where my firewoman rendered first aid. The injured man was badly burned about the face, and later removed to the Middlesex Hospital.

Branches were now in position and the fire was well surrounded.

When the situation at the BBC appeared to be in hand, the superintendent returned to his district control at Manchester Square Fire Station where he learnt that an AFS sub-station in Chelsea had received a direct hit, with one fireman dead, several injured and one still missing:

Whilst on my way, when turning out of Grosvenor Square, with my dispatch rider following close behind me, a stick of three bombs came whistling down. One struck a building one hundred yards in our rear and in a flash the dispatch rider shot past the car at about sixty miles per hour. The next bomb dropped in front of us, and in the flash of the burst I could see the coping stones leaving the building as we were passing. The third bomb of the stick dropped ahead of us in Hyde Park, near the gun sites. When we turned into Park Lane, I signalled the dispatch rider to stop, and upon inquiring why he had increased speed and passed us, he stated that it had not been of his own volition, but was caused by the blast of the exploding bomb.

When I arrived at the sub-station in Chelsea, I found that a large bomb had demolished a corner block of flats and had severely blasted the station. The dead fireman had been removed and the injured were receiving attention from a first aid party. The missing man had not been located, so after making some inquiries, I commenced a personal search of the area. About two hundred yards from the station, I found a steel helmet, and, lying face downwards in the gutter about twenty yards from the spot, under coping stones and debris, I found the missing man. There was no doubt that he was dead.

The fire officer went on to visit large fires in the Pimlico area and witnessed an amazing sight. In the middle of a mass of devastation was a large bomb crater almost full of water, a gas main burning furiously nearby, and the entire scene lit by hundreds of fires all around. At the edge of the bomb crater, sitting in shirt sleeves with feet dangling in the water, was an AFS fireman calmly clearing out the strainers of two nearby trailer pumps. He thought that they had become blocked by debris in the crater and seemed totally oblivious of everything around him: the fires, the anti-aircraft gunfire, the falling bombs. In fact the strainers were not blocked—the problem was water turbulence in the crater as vast quantities of street-surface water from other fire-fighting jets poured back into the hole. So the pump suctions were repositioned and water was set flowing again through the hoses to the waiting firemen at the branches.

That night, a large part of the West End was badly hit as showers of incendiaries continued to fall. Christ Church, in Westminster, was alight from end to end and a ten-storied building in Petty France was also set ablaze. A solitary trailer pump and crew arrived to deal with the church and several minutes later two similar pumps arrived just down the road in Petty France. There was some water available in the street hydrants but the fire situation was hopeless. Eventually a turntable ladder arrived and was set up to aim a water jet at the roof of Christ Church. Hardly had it been positioned and a water supply connected to it, when the turntable ladder was hit by a stick of bombs. One fireman was killed instantly and seven others seriously injured, two of whom died subsequently. The fireman 100ft up at the top of the ladder, as in the September 1940 Great Portland Street incident, had an amazing escape. When the bombs fell the ladder remained basically intact, being blown against the parapet of the church. The fireman at the top was knocked unconscious. Amid the chaos and carnage below he appeared to be completely forgotten; after several minutes he regained consciousness, unhooked himself and was able to make his own faltering way down to street level. The man was badly shocked and suffered cuts and bruises, but insisted on remaining at the scene.

Selfridge's in Oxford Street also suffered a direct hit and the first officer to arrive asked for fifty pumps. There was already a one-hundred pump incident going on at the Marylebone goods yard of the London and North Eastern Railway, less than a mile away. A water relay was installed using the 6in steel pipeline, with water being pumped from the Serpentine to Marble Arch and from there by multiple lines of hose into dams along Oxford Street to feed the dozens of pumps ready to receive the precious supply.

Although provision of fire watchers was now compulsory, many understandably took cover during the raids and fires were able to develop undetected. Around midnight, a batch of incendiaries fell on a large block of offices just off Oxford Street and within five minutes the entire corner section was alight along the roof and on several floors. Before the first pump of the over-burdened LFS arrived, some army officers, with the best of intentions, had broken open various doors in the hope of doing some useful work. The resulting draughts and cross-currents of air fanned the flames higher and more fiercely than ever. The LFS fought the fire all night. In the middle of it there was a terrific explosion from the vortex of fire in the heart of the building. Nobody could explain it, for no bursting boiler could have sent the flames and debris so high. Days after, when the demolition workers were clearing up, the reason was discovered. Buried under the bricks and twisted girders were the remains of a burnt-out German bomber.

At about 3am, Auxiliary Fireman William Sansom and three others of a solitary crew were at work with their jets along the front face of a blazing five-storey City warehouse, when suddenly the complete front wall of the building began to fall outwards onto the firemen. Sansom later recalled:

A wall will fall in many ways. It may sway over to the one side or the other. It may crumble at the very beginning of its fall. It may remain intact and fall flat. This wall fell as flat as a pancake. It clung to its shape through forty-five degrees to the horizontal. Then it detached itself from the pivot and slammed down on top of us.

The last resistance of bricks and mortar at the pivot point cracked off like automatic gunfire. The violent sound both deafened and brought us to our senses. We dropped the hose and crouched. Afterwards Verno said that I knelt slowly on one knee with bowed head, like a man about to be knighted. Well, I got my knighting. There was an incredible noise—a thunder-clap condensed into the space of an eardrum—and then the bricks and the mortar came tearing and burning into the flesh of my face.

Lofty, away by the pump, was killed. Len, Verno and myself they dug out. There was very little brick on top of us. We had been lucky. We had been framed by one of those symmetrical, oblong window spaces.

A woman's view of such a night is interesting. As a part-time watchroom attendant at a central London sub-station, Auxiliary Firewoman Owtram recalled:

The control room is small. It has the width of a medium-wide passage. It contains four chairs, the control table, on which stand the telephones, and a smaller table. There are boards and maps, on which discs are hung, on the walls. The window is bricked up. The lights are harsh. The atmosphere is blue with the smoke, which cannot escape, of past hours. In fact, the control room disproves the theory that mammals require air in which to breathe. There are two AFS girls and the mobilizing officer on duty. The telephones do not cease to ring nor the slips, almost every one of which represents a fire, to be stabbed in order upon the file. I take my place. The girl whom I am relieving vanishes at once. The mobilizing officer, speaking from behind me, says:

'Send a pump to John Mercer's premises, Goley Street, Thames Wharf.' I transmit the order.

And so the night—very noisy—wears on. It may be that, in two more hours, every pump will have trickled back, all the fires be under control . . . Or it may be that the drain of pumps from our station and from the five sub-stations under us will not have been replaced by returning pumps nor by pumps reinforcing from other areas whose drivers loom dramatic in the doorway with 'Harrow' painted white upon their tin hats, or 'Chipping Ongar' or 'Slough'.

On the night of which I am thinking, all our pumps were out. We had no more to send. This situation led to a lull in the control room, though not in the raid. The other AFS girl on duty lay down on a stretcher-bed to snatch a little rest. The mobilizing officer and I smoked and ate toast and drank tea. We discussed continental cooking. We also discussed the houseproud lives of the women of Scandinavia and whether they were not happier in those lives than the more restless young women of our own country. We thought that, on the whole, they might be. 'But you can't,' we solemnly agreed, 'put the clock back.' Though whether either of us believed this last statement, I do not know.

The hours passed. No pump returned. A glance at the board would show you where they were: 'Location of Fire', said the neat lettering, after which the address was written in chalk. In due course the other AFS girl was prodded awake. I took her place upon the bed, wrapping myself in my blanket. I felt like a soldier, but I did not sleep, not having the courage which would enable me to do so while that heavy droning filled the sky. This sound died from the heavens at last. I heard the telephone ring. I heard the message given to all sub-stations: 'Air-raid message White.'

Then came the long, high, certain, sweet note of the 'all-clear'.

At seven o'clock, as I went home, no pump had yet returned.

The darkness of the street, after the glare of the control room, seemed, for a moment, like a wall against which one would strike oneself. The sky in the east was a bitter red which might have been the dawn but wasn't. Our pumps would be there, no doubt, and a hundred others. The men would be black to the eyes, hungry, frozen and soaking wet.

I felt the wind that cut at my face and hands. I felt the longing for sleep, to which, so soon, I could yield; and to which the men at the pumps couldn't yield—perhaps, for hours. I felt delight that the perils of the night were at an end. And most of all, I felt—as I still feel—pride at being connected, however lightly, with so proud a service.

Many pumps and crews were still damping down fires when dawn came. In spite of the deployment of canteen vans, men had been manning branches for hours on end with no relief for refreshment. All 2,300 incidents were under control by mid-morning the next day, but the night had cost London dearly—1,108 men, women and children lay dead and over 2,000 were seriously injured.

Another severe raid followed three nights later, but although heavy and prolonged it was not on the same scale. Most affected were the East End, East and West Ham, Barking and a number of widespread districts of south-east London and the suburbs. LFS crews and local brigades were able to meet the demands of the night without recourse to outside regional assistance, even though there were precious few pumps in reserve.

In late April, the Luftwaffe raided Plymouth for five nights and in the first days of May, Merseyside was at the mercy of the enemy for seven nights on end. Both these cities received help from the LFS. A convoy of thirty pumps was also sent to Birmingham to provide fire cover there, for a large number of Birmingham's own appliances had gone to the aid of Merseyside. While the London crews were away, the capital was thankfully spared regular nightly raids. The majority of on-duty personnel were able to rest at their stations, to drink endless cups of tea, play cards or just chat. To unwind properly was difficult for most and sleep was only deep and sustaining after the tremendous physical exertions of a major raid. Whilst the Luftwaffe struck at the ports and northern cities, the lull over London did not allow the LFS to relax fully. The appliances and firemen were ready to go at half a minute's notice, their state of readiness never in doubt. But a progressive tiredness was beginning to build up amongst the personnel, and this was greatly exacerbated in many cases by the strain of waiting for any further raids that might come.

As the spring of 1941 blossomed into May, the future looked uncertain and ominous. There was every prospect of more aerial battering and of a continuing test of the courage, spirit and resilience of the weary men and women who manned the thin line of London's fire defences.

8

The Last Major Fire Raid

Saturday, 10 May 1941, dawned cold and clear. It was Cup Final day—Arsenal v Preston North End at Wembley. By 3pm, 60,000 supporters were yelling their lungs out in enthusiastic support of their team. For most, and particularly the Londoners, the war seemed far away. There had been no air-raids over the London region for four weeks and war on the home front had quietened down, although the intermittent raiding of some ports had continued into early May.

As the Wembley crowd cheered over the excitement of an end-to-end game, a single telephone call from the HQ of RAF fighter command to Major Jackson's office at fire service headquarters, Lambeth, gave the first hint of what was to come. The call simply said that the RAF monitoring unit had established that the powerful radio beams along which the bombers of the Luftwaffe navigated towards a target, were set to intersect over West Ham.

Jackson, as the commander of the LFS, was on duty this weekend and he personally rang the Home Office Fire Control across the river in Whitehall. Jackson asked that 1,000 pumps stand by on the fringes of London. His immediate concern was that the LFS should be as ready as possible. The Home Office, however, were not easily convinced that this was to be a fire raid, or even a raid at all. With blitz fires still burning in Hull and Liverpool, the Home Office staff had an immensely difficult task in organising supporting men and appliances. To commit such numbers to London as Jackson was requesting was a gamble. The chief of fire staff at the Home Office, Commander Firebrace, knew the problems.

As pre-war chief of the LFB he had a clear knowledge of the City's fire risks, and must have been more than sympathetic towards this enormous request for pumps from his previous deputy. He had spent much of his time during the earlier London blitzes in the streets alongside firemen, seeing just how well his own mobilisation scheme was working.

Firebrace compromised with Jackson and agreed that 750 pumps would be mobilised from outer regions into London as soon as possible. The arithmetic was simple. On this night there were some 1,270 pumps available in the London County Council area of London and a further 1,242 ready in the outer regions. These included appliances from the various brigades in Middlesex, Hertfordshire, Essex, Kent, Surrey and Sussex, as well as the county boroughs which included West and East Ham, and Croydon. Thus a potential total of 2,500 pumps would be available if the threatened raid developed. However, on the night of the City raid of 29 December 1940 all these had been in action and 300 outer region appliances had been needed. That had been an attack on a relatively concentrated district. During the big, wider raid of 16 April 1941, with over 2,200 fires logged, many of the hundreds of moderate-size fires required as many as ten pumps each to achieve control. Hence Jackson's understandable request which leant towards 'better too many than too few'.

As night fell, there was still no 'red' alert. For the several thousand firemen 'standing to' at their stations across London, the minutes ticked by and the telephones to Lambeth and the street fire-alarm panels in the watchrooms remained silent. Through the length and breadth of its outer suburbs, London's wardens pressed on with their nightly house-to-house patrol, always with an eye and an ear to the sky.

There was a full moon on this May night and its clear silvery light was reflected on the dropping waters of the Thames, greater expanses of wet mud being revealed as the fast-ebbing tide slipped away. By 10.30pm, there seemed little water left in London's river. This was not the lowest possible tide at that time of year, but it was not far off it. That night the tide had dropped 18ft below the high water level mark. Access for pumps to the available water at such low tides was across about 50ft of deep treacherous mud on either side of the Thames.

Around 10.45pm, the first twenty Luftwaffe bombers steering along one of the radio beams, had crossed the Channel. Almost simultaneously radar stations along the South Coast were picking up further mass bleeps as enemy aircraft took to the sky from twenty airfields in France, Belgium and Holland. Half an hour later, there was little doubt as to the target. It looked as if London was to suffer a massive raid. As the sirens on the rooftops of police stations across the entire capital and the suburbs accelerated into their wailing tones, the first of the incendiaries were falling; not only on West Ham but on a front nearly ten miles long from Barking to the edge of the City. Many old targets were hit again, including the Royal Group of Docks at Silvertown and Surrey Docks and the timber wharves. Over the next half an hour, as progressive waves of bombers showered down their incendiary and high-explosive loads, it was evident that this was to be a fire raid of horrendous proportions.

ENCROACHING HOLOCAUST

Within a short time of the raid starting, fires in the West Ham area alone appeared to have absorbed all the available pumps in the vicinity, and the West Ham chief, Herbert Johnson, was asking for more. Jackson, concerned that the raid might well develop further westwards, took himself off to West Ham to see the situation at first-hand: he wanted to ensure that every appliance was being used to advantage. When Jackson arrived at West Ham HQ he discovered that Johnson had over-ordered pumps and was not deploying many of those at his disposal, saying that he wanted some held in reserve. Jackson hurriedly dispatched the waiting appliances

towards Whitechapel and the glow from fires being left unattended by the fire service. Each of Jackson's senior officers
were now at the scene of a major fire area, attempting to
control and co-ordinate the men and pumps that seemed to
arrive in woefully small numbers.

At Home Office Fire Control, the 750 pumps promised
hours earlier to Jackson were slow in being mobilised; many
of the 1,600 local brigades in the UK were independent in the
real sense of the word. Almost ten months into the fire-
fighters' war, many smaller brigades had been little affected
by the blitz. Urgent phone calls during the evening to these
small units brought a variety of excuses why they could not
support the capital in its night of dire need . . . the mayor
would have to sanction the move first; the appliance had a list
of defects; the personnel were not available for these duties . . .
For the hard-pressed staff at Firebrace's HQ it was an uphill
task, and all the time the bombers were spreading their load
over a widening area of London in a continuous and concentrated pattern.

Paradoxically, the first fire-service convoy to set out for
London that night was formed entirely of London men and
pumps. Fifty LFS appliances which had been supporting
Birmingham after a week of raiding in the northern cities
were recalled, and were mobile by midnight. By then the raid
over London was at its pitch. As the raid moved over the
central area of London, the British Museum was hit and
although the art treasures had been removed, the roof of the
building was fiercely alight. St Pancras railway station lost
most of the glass in its sweeping roof-span and a huge bomb
crater in the station itself exposed the underground track
of the Metropolitan line below. Fires in Clerkenwell warehouses and in the City were spreading and by 12.25am all
telephone links with the City, Holborn, Shoreditch and
Bethnal Green were severed.

The bombing had already damaged many strategic water
mains, including the principal City trunk main connecting

the Thames near Cannon Street railway station to City Road. The West End main joining the Grand Union Canal at Regent's Park to Shaftesbury Avenue in theatreland was also out of action. Both of these were vital to fire-fighting operations.

Back at Lambeth, Jackson could see the position developing and becoming graver by the minute. Unlike the relatively localised raids of September to December 1940, and March the following year, this raid was already widespread. The large wall plots showing the situation indicated major fires from the eastern and southern boundaries to the centre. News came continually of more problems of breakdown in communications, lack of water supplies and not enough pumps to attend all the initial calls, let alone the cries for additional help.

A warehouse next to the LFS 'B' district headquarters in Rosebery Avenue, Clerkenwell, received a direct hit. 'B' district covered the high-risk City of London, Shoreditch and Whitechapel areas, and suddenly seventy-five sub-stations were cut off from their mobilising control. Clerkenwell had no idea where to send reinforcing pumps as they arrived at 'B' division HQ, or what the fire situation was in any particular district. Dispatch riders were hastily commandeered, but valuable time was lost before some vestige of contact and control was re-established between Clerkenwell Control, its stations and Lambeth HQ.

A FRIGHTENING PICTURE

Auxiliary Fireman Henry Stedman remembered going to a fire reported in a warehouse in the vicinity of Cannon Street:

No words can describe the inferno that raged in London that night. Overhead was the ceaseless drone of the bombers, the air was rent by thud after thud of heavy bombs, mixed up with the rattle of the incendiaries that almost rained down. Acting as accompaniment to the already indescribable din was the ceaseless roar and rattle of our anti-aircraft guns hurling their destructive little shells up into the sky which had become one giant pattern of weaving searchlights. Once or twice we thought we heard, above the general din, the scream of a racing aero-engine as a night fighter dived steeply to attack a something that, to its pilot, could only be a dim shape in the darkness.

For a good half mile the road was covered by broken and shattered glass that fell like cataracts from every window in the street.

Our destination was the Cannon Street district, and, as we passed one fire after another, we knew we were in for a busy night. Close to the railway station we saw a rather unnerving sight, a huge bomb crater that stretched almost across the road-way, and lying in the bottom, twisted and buckled almost beyond recognition, a tender with its pump. Without hope we speculated on the fate of its unfortunate crew.

More than once on that journey we ducked our heads as we heard the swishing noise of a bomb coming rapidly downwards at a steep angle to end up with a sickening crump in a block of buildings or bury itself in the roadway behind us.

Once at the scene, Stedman's crew found a roaring fire being tackled by a few men with several trailer pumps and nowhere near enough water:

But inadequate or not they were doing their best, and we wasted no time in adding our jets to those already playing on to the flames.

Within half an hour I was soaked to the skin with the water that streamed backwards from the walls and roof of the building; the pressure in our branch was very considerable and it took two of us all our time to hold it in position at all. Only those who have actually experienced it realise the tremendous backward drag there is on a line of live hose. The time slipped slowly by, and, as the night came on, I got colder and colder in my soaked clothing, few other pumps came to assist us, and gradually, despite our most desperate efforts, it became obvious that the building would be entirely gutted.

It was certainly a cold night—one degree below zero at mid-night—the coldest May night since records were kept. Another hazard was the number of delayed-action parachute mines being dropped. Earlier, thirty-eight of these had fallen on West Ham alone and others fell over a wider area, including most of the districts heavily affected by fire.

At headquarters, the overall picture of the raid was frightening. At one stage, soon after midnight, the AFS women operators in the central control room logged no fewer than six potential conflagrations in eighteen minutes, including one at the Elephant and Castle. Fires were burning virtually unchecked in Farmiloes paint works, Battersea, in the Cable and Wireless head office in Moorgate, and in Gordon's Gin distillery in the City Road. Queen Victoria Street from Cannon Street down to the Blackfriars end, was one growing sheet of flame and the few firemen on the scene had no water at all to feed their waiting pumps. As on the night of 29 December, many historic buildings burned, including the Temple Church, Sergeant's Inn and several Wren churches.

Many of London's main-line railway termini had already been badly hit; below the platforms of Waterloo Station a fearsome fire was developing in the vaults, threatening the vast station complex above. Everywhere firemen were continually met with entreaties from wardens and police to hurriedly bring their equipment to staunch fresh fires. Householders braved the bombs, pleading with the firemen to leave all other fires and deal with their own precious homes and possessions. But the priorities were clear and wherever possible, buildings of national importance—hospitals, those involved with the war effort, and premises with a high life risk—had first call on the LFS. Others could not expect an immediate response.

INVIDIOUS DECISIONS

It was a frustrating experience for the fire crews in the streets who had to withstand pleas for help, but they stood their ground. Even worse was the situation facing the pump crews en route to a fire area; some of them found themselves almost stopped and overwhelmed by people running out into

the road thinking that the appliance was destined to come to
their aid rather than going to a fire perhaps still a mile or so
distant.

A crew of eight firemen were tackling a blaze in the roof of
St Thomas's Hospital opposite the Houses of Parliament
when a breathless verger ran up. He said that the roof of
nearby Lambeth Palace was alight and that the archbishop
was in residence. Would the officer-in-charge please come.
But the officer knew that no fresh help was immediately
available and that the hospital fire had yet to be beaten. Such
decisions were constantly being made by both fire officers
and firemen, irrespective of the occupants of a building,
even if one happened to be an archbishop.

When a fire call was received to the roof of Buckingham
Palace soon after midnight, several pumps were mobilised
and quickly arrived from nearby sub-stations. They found
the palace gates locked and bolted; it seemed that the usual
Metropolitan Police gate-officers had wisely taken cover
during the raid, for they were nowhere to be seen. The Royal
Family were at Windsor that weekend and although no fire
or smoke was evident, principal officer Clement Kerr decided
that this was no time to stand on ceremony. Kerr climbed the
lofty railings enclosing the palace forecourt telling his men to
follow, and, two at a time, the group of London firemen
gained this improbable entry into the sovereign's London
residence unchallenged. They made their way into the
palace and climbed to the upper floors where Kerr found
no apparent fire but evidence of some scorching in a corner
of the roof. The crews left as they had entered the palace
and the origin of the call was never clearly established.

No sooner had Kerr dealt with that alarm, than a dispatch
rider brought word of a serious roof fire at the Palace of
Westminster, which collectively included the House of Lords,
House of Commons and Westminster Hall. When Kerr
arrived several minutes later he found pump crews waiting to
gain access to the building. The Palace of Westminster fire

watchers consisted of twelve Metropolitan policemen, not the palace's own staff, and there was some delay in finding the keys to allow the fire-fighters to get up the narrow stone staircases to the upper roof. As the correct keys to the heavy oak doors were hurriedly sorted out, more incendiaries dropped and ignited on the roof of Westminster Hall close by. Across the square, Westminster Abbey was getting the same treatment and flames already had a strong hold on one corner of the abbey roof. The first trailer pump pulled up outside the abbey just before 1am, when the raid seemed to be at its greatest intensity.

Soon after 1am, Major Jackson surveyed the scene at his London headquarters. By now hardly any of the 2,500 pumps originally pooled were ready to respond to the calls still streaming in, most of them now going unanswered. Jackson called Home Office Control and demanded the latest news on the outer regional pumps promised earlier. Only a few had so far reached London and been put to work. The crews from the outer Home Counties were at a great disadvantage. They could hardly be expected to know the geography of any London district particularly well, let alone the configurations of the major buildings, the layout of hydrants and the availability of emergency water supplies. Worse still, much of their equipment, including hose couplings, often did not match that used by the LFS and the supporting crews had to work as individual units, rather than as part of a collective fire-fighting team. With the bombers still overhead in a seemingly endless stream, Jackson knew that London was facing a crisis.

Nowhere was this clearer than at the Elephant and Castle, in south London, where a whole range of fires had begun to join up into a ringed area of angry flame. The streets bounded by Walworth Road, New Kent Road, Newington Butts and Causeway were becoming one almost impenetrable raging mass of fire. Every hydrant around was dry and ten more pumps had been asked for, in addition to those sent when the first calls were received soon after midnight. The senior officer in charge at the Elephant and Castle was a realist. At that moment he could have used a hundred pumps but knew that such strength was just not around. By 12.15am, he and his men were dealing with a fire that had already engulfed five acres of buildings and was spreading in all directions. All the major water mains had suffered under the tremendous blows of the bombing and the four pump crews sent in each direction to search for undamaged hydrants returned to the Elephant to report little success.

Elsewhere things looked equally grim. The raid seemed if anything to be spreading farther westward, over central London. Kensington, Paddington and St Marylebone were now experiencing concentrated falls of high explosives and incendiaries. All the main-line railway termini except Marylebone had been hit, and the fire in the vaults of Waterloo Station was still burning unchecked. At the Theobalds Road end of the City, crews were so hard-pressed for water that manhole covers were lifted and for a short while water was pumped from the sewers below. It was not long, however, before the fine mesh of the strainers fitted at the ends of the suction hose became clogged and clearing these was an extremely unpleasant task.

Not far away, an AFS crew had made a jet work from a trailer pump by dropping the pump's suction hose into a deep water-filled bomb crater. The water was probably entering the crater through the subsoil from a broken main close by, but within ten minutes the pump output overtook it. As the level of the water dropped, there slowly broke surface the unmistakable shape of the tail fin of an unexploded 500lb bomb lying nose-down in the crater. Ever since the pump had started up, its suction hose had been vibrating against the bomb in the water and it was a wise fireman who shut down his pump and quickly made off to find his mates. It is not recorded if they believed his story.

Communication became more difficult as the night wore

on and even dispatch riders had difficulty getting their messages through. Every link over the Thames from London Bridge to Lambeth was badly damaged and hundreds of gutted buildings had partially collapsed outwards, blocking thoroughfares. Seven hundred gas mains were fractured and burned fiercely, adding clarity to the Luftwaffe's target.

Twenty pumps, including some from the outer regions, had been ordered to rendezvous in a narrow street north of Holborn Viaduct station. Since that order had been given, the fires at this spot had worsened and all the parked pumps not yet in use were themselves threatened by the flames, red-hot debris and settling sparks. Before these valuable appliances could be moved out, the fall of a nearby wall caused a flurry of burning fragments to cascade over several of the pumps, and the petrol tank of one caught fire. All the firemen beat a hasty retreat but were unable to recover any of the appliances as they burst into flames from the blistering heat. All twenty pumps were lost.

HELP FROM ESSEX

Of all the augmenting fire-fighters coming into the capital on this dramatic night, the experiences of one crew from Essex were typical.

Nobby Clark was an AFS leading fireman with the Benfleet Volunteer Fire Brigade, stationed at Hadleigh in Essex. He joined the AFS several months before the outbreak of war and had already seen a fair amount of action in and around the South Essex area as a result of air-raids. Pumps from Clark's area had travelled to the capital to provide help during the City raid of 29 December 1940. On that occasion Clark and his colleagues had been deployed at several huge fires near the Tower of London for ten hours of strenuous fire-fighting with, as usual, hardly any water.

When the telephone rang at Hadleigh Fire Station at 9pm on the night of 10 May 1941 with the urgent request from

London Fire Control, Clark could envisage what the Essex firemen might be heading for. Six pumps were soon on the road for London, led by Clark who was in charge of the Hadleigh appliance. He had a particularly good knowledge of the London area and had acted as convoy leader on the night of the City raid.

The small convoy made away from the Thames and the ever-present threat from strafing enemy fighters. As they passed the Purfleet and Grays districts, large fires were burning from earlier raids. Further on at Dagenham, they encountered clouds of heavy smoke in the night air, and once beyond this hazard large blazes were again clearly visible in all directions. Approaching Romford the main road was lit almost as bright as day with the light from fires burning on either side. Most of these were already being dealt with by local fire-fighting units.

At Ilford things seemed a little quieter, until a police constable stepped into the road and abruptly halted the convoy. He informed Clark that several unexploded bombs had closed main roads ahead. Undeterred, Clark used a short detour and soon had the six pumps heading due west again for London. The original orders were to report initially to Whitechapel Fire Station, but as the convoy approached West Ham, still some 4 miles from Whitechapel, Clark could see that the fire situation all around was dire. He therefore halted the line of pumps outside the Stratford Fire Station of the West Ham Fire Brigade. The station itself was devoid of pumps and firemen, but soon after their arrival a West Ham officer arrived in a staff car and detached three of the Essex appliances and their crews for work in the immediate area. Clark was instructed to proceed as ordered and told that a large flour mill further west at Bow Bridge was ablaze and out of control. One more Essex pump was to be left to assist there and the diminished convoy was then to press on towards Whitechapel. When, minutes later, Clark stopped his remaining three pumps near the blazing mill, the local fire officer ran up and promptly commandeered two of the appliances.

Clark, now understandably left feeling somewhat lonely with his single pump and crew of seven men, carried on towards central London. As they drove up Whitechapel Road towards Aldgate and the City, they noticed the quantities of hose laid across the streets, and the night sky on their left over the Thames was like an orange dawn. The 30-odd miles from Hadleigh had taken almost three hours to travel. Clark went inside the bomb-damaged Whitechapel Fire Station to report to the district control. Like Stratford, Whitechapel was empty of pumps, although several dispatch riders were coming and going with messages from not-too-distant fires. Occasionally an appliance clanged urgently past as the Essex firemen waited anxiously for news of their destination. Clark's pump was quickly ordered to report to the mobile control set up at Mansion House. Once they had carefully negotiated Aldgate and Fenchurch Street, the crew saw that they were now entering the real battle zone of a fire area. Dozens of hoses led along each street, alleyway and courtyard. Fallen debris lay everywhere and large burning fragments of fire drifted around with the warm wind like fiery dandelions, reluctant to settle on the pavements of the near-deserted city. Bombs were falling in a steady pattern, their explosions regularly jarring roads and pavements with a monotony that was both frightening and frustrating.

Once at the Mansion House, Clark was unable to locate the control unit amid the mêlée of hose and firemen struggling to get to work in all directions. An LFB officer appeared and breathlessly told him that the control point had been moved back to another position. The Hadleigh crew were to set their pump into a 5,000-gallon static tank which was being fed by a relay previously laid from King William Street by a hose-laying lorry.

Glad to have some fire-fighting to do after this long trail up to London, they duly dropped the suction hose into the water supply and ran out the coils of hose from their pump towards burning buildings on each side of Queen Victoria Street. Each man felt the effect of the tremendous heat waves from the intense fires as they progressively worked nearer the infernos. Within minutes, the Hadleigh driver had his pump engine running and primed. Once the water started to course along the limp hose lines the Essex firemen at each end of the branches braced themselves, as their jets crackled and hissed into life. Of the three jets they could provide, two were trained into the heart of fires and the third was directed against premises almost opposite and as yet unaffected. When in contact with the frontage the water stream quickly turned into clouds of steam; so hot was the face of the building from radiated heat that the paint on the windows and doors continued bubbling and smoking despite the effect of the cooling water. Clark recalled the conditions of that awful night:

I looked along the street and saw other pumps at work, including a turntable ladder working at about 100ft at the far end of the Salvation Army building which was well alight on all floors. We heard aircraft coming and soon after bombs fell around, starting more fires. Across the river towards Southwark a large area literally burst into flame and spread rapidly. Then I noticed all the jets along Queen Victoria Street start to dry up. Looking round I saw ours begin to fail also, so I shut them all down except the one cooling jet. No water was coming through to the static water tank which was now less than half full, so I reduced the jet nozzle size to conserve what water there was and sent three men back along the relay to investigate. Each man was told not to separate or venture too far afield. Seeing my cooling jet still working, an LFB officer came along and asked how much water I had. I replied not much, although there was a large unopened hydrant nearby. This was opened up, but nothing came out at all, despite the fact that it was a twenty-five inch main.

Suddenly the whole front of the burning Salvation Army building collapsed into the street, completely blocking the road. The turntable ladder was still standing erect, surrounded by a heap of rubble. Many firemen ran towards the scene and started getting injured fire-fighters out of the chaos. All my hose was buried under red-hot rubble. My other three crew members came back safely and realizing the position was now untenable, I got them to start making up what hose they could in spite of the heat from the debris behind us.

The heat was terrific and I soon felt dazed and giddy and was violently sick. I seemed unable to think and felt the strange urge to walk towards the heat. It was as if I had no weight in my body at all. How long I remained like that I do not know, but the rest of the crew said afterwards that they had felt much the same. Then I realized that somebody had at last found some more water. Two officers appeared with some men pulling a trailer pump. We got the pump to work with two jets and soon after I was told to take my pump and crew to Clerkenwell via Finsbury Square; there was to be a complete evacuation of Queen Victoria Street and surrounding area. As we entered Threadneedle Street I saw a group of firemen emerging from the underground station. Some of these men were being carried. I stopped the pump and ran back to them. They told me that most of the water mains where they had been working had been knocked out by the last lot of bombs. They had been cut off by fire and had made their escape through the tube tunnel. My crew packed them on the back of the appliance and I moved on. When we reached Finsbury Square, I unloaded all but my own crew as there was a control unit in position and some first aid available.

We went on by way of Old Street and then down Clerkenwell Road. At the junction with Farringdon Road, I was flagged down by an LFB officer. He told us to get to work from a large water dam that actually had a good supply of water pouring into it. Somewhat wearily, we got four jets to work from this supply to attempt to prevent the spread of fire from a nearby warehouse that was alight from top to bottom.

It was several hours later when we were relieved by another heavy pump unit and crew from some outer London station. After recovering what we could of our precious hose, we were ordered to a sub-station in Clerkenwell for a meal. Before the war the sub-station had been a school and as my crew ate ravenously in the dining hall, there was hardly any talk at all. We were utterly worn out. For some time we watched other convoys arriving and being ordered straight on to the fire zones. Apparently water supplies were gradually being restored and the frontal attack was being pushed steadily forward.

About 3.30pm, all officers in charge of pumps were called to the station watch room. A senior LFB officer stood in the centre of the room with a pile of nominal roll boards which showed the names of each pump crew. He called out my name and asked where I came from; I replied the Southend area and after he had inquired where we had worked during the night and morning, the officer said that he thought we had done enough and could get off home.

We headed off at a steady pace and stopped in Romford for a cup of tea. Several large convoys passed us going in the other direction, towards London. We arrived back at Hadleigh at about 6pm.

The fire-fighters from Essex had been away in London for over twenty-one wearying hours without respite. They thankfully had a quick wash and grabbed a few hours sleep in their fire station. Within ten hours they were back in convoy, bound for London yet again.

DISASTER AT THE ELEPHANT AND CASTLE

The rescue of people buried alive in partially collapsed buildings was also difficult. Such work was normally the special task of the heavy rescue gangs of the Civil Defence. By 2am that morning, there were over 150 'persons trapped' incidents in the London County Council area alone and many of them were close to major fires, which proved extremely trying for rescue crews. Their technique involved careful digging into an area of rubble where it was suspected someone was buried, then calling for a brief spell of complete silence during which they listened for any cries, moans or groans to guide their efforts. In practice, a pause for silence was impossible during a raid, with bombs falling and the general cacophony of fire-fighting sounds nearby, particularly pumps roaring away for hours on end.

At the Elephant and Castle, more pumps had arrived but there was still a chronic shortage of water. The fire-fighting situation there was in the hands of Divisional Officer G. V.

Blackstone, one of Jackson's highly experienced cadre of LFB senior officers. For months before this raid Blackstone had been nagging the architects' department of the London County Council about the need to instal further static water supplies. They in turn disagreed, preferring to rely on the few large reservoirs around the London area. Blackstone and his immediate superior, John Fordham, had grown tired of haggling at County Hall and taken unilateral action. During the lull of the winter months, the two officers had identified the large basement of the blitzed Surrey Music Hall at the Elephant and Castle as being an ideal emergency water reservoir. Crews of firemen cemented the inside of the basement and had it filled with almost a quarter of a million gallons of water. When officials at County Hall found out a short time after, they labelled the fire service action 'unconstitutional'.

As firemen scouted around the area, searching in vain for water, Blackstone was able to get pumps in position to draw water from the music-hall basement and this work progressed swiftly. The contents of two local swimming-baths were already in use but could not last much longer. Five hundred firemen were now at the Elephant fire and many were frantically engaged in laying the first of several water relays to bring distant supplies to the endangered area. The relays were laid from the Thames at London, Waterloo and Westminster Bridges using hose-laying lorries, but it was a time-consuming process. At the relay source, the Thames was still very low and somehow the 50ft wide mud banks had to be crossed to get pumps close enough to draw up the water.

The water from the music-hall reservoir was much more rapid in coming through and hose lines were soon pouring it into smaller dams. From here other pumps began to charge hoses whose branches were manned by waiting firemen. All around the fire area, men cowered from the awful heat of the raging inferno as jet after jet went into action. Great showers of sparks fell continually like gently falling rain and the bombs were still falling with some intensity.

Water from the vital music-hall source had only been coming through for a short while when a high-explosive bomb fell right onto one of the pumps supplying the water. This appliance and also the others nearby were literally blown apart and large parts of the pumps were scattered over a wide area. When the dust cloud settled, twelve firemen lay dead amid the debris and the basement reservoir had been made completely inaccessible.

Fortunately for Fordham and Blackstone, water from the 3½in diameter hose relay from London Bridge over a mile away was now beginning to come through and a number of jets were fed from that supply. These started to isolate the fire. As a message for a further fifty pumps was hurriedly dispatched, the more experienced fire-fighters at the Elephant and Castle sensed the draught created by the vast amounts of air being drawn into the conflagration. It did not augur well for the struggling firemen.

Fires around St Paul's were also giving Major Jackson great cause for concern. Although by 3am the fall of incendiaries over the City of London had eased, a number of unattended fires around the cathedral were spreading at an alarming rate. The streets between St Paul's and the river front were becoming one great fire and those to the north, east and west were little better. One of the hundreds of threatened premises was Faraday Building in Queen Victoria Street, midway between St Paul's and Blackfriars; this housed both the Continental telephone exchange and the overseas radio link with the Commonwealth and the United States, and was of prime strategic importance.

The various water relays from the Thames were the fire-fighters' key to success, but laying the 3½in diameter hose was only part of the problem. All along the routes of relays to the worst fires at the Elephant and Castle, St Paul's, Whitechapel and Westminster, collapsing buildings and red-hot stonework, bricks and roof timbers fell across the lines of hose. Whole crews of firemen were organised continually to patrol the lines to try to keep the water flowing once it was coming through: because of many such obstructions, some relays had to be stopped and partially relaid. By 5am, nine miles of hose were delivering water to the Elephant and Castle fire zone.

The men at work on the fireboats out in the Thames had a grandstand view of the burning of London. Ever since the raid began they had plied up and down the river, occasionally using the powerful water jets on their own fireboats to quell a waterfront blaze. Others laid their small vessels under the bridges or just off the mud, in some cases feeding 4 tons of water per minute on to the shore and towards the fires. Auxiliary Fireman Dewsbury Dessau was a crew member on a fireboat at work just below the St Paul's riverline:

The first time I saw it, it was coming under Blackfriars Bridge. Scorched brown and horrible with burnt hair and what looked like elbows. Bob-bobbing up and down with the wavering tide.

What got me most was that this thing had no head. I'd seen bodies before—shrivelled and shrunk and burnt like this— down at the docks fires, but they'd always had a head. My breath sucked in, and there was a sudden prickly cold about my ears, spiking up under my tin hat. I shuddered a bit and took my eyes off it.

I had twenty cans of petrol ready on the cabin-top as we slewed, nose pointing upstream, and oy-oyed as we slooshed alongside another fireboat. A weary fireman lumbered over the stern lockers, begrimed and ungainly in his oilskins, and yanked up the petrol as I held it out, one can at a time. A flash split the gloom while he was taking the chocolate rations, and his eyes, I saw, were red-rimmed from lack of sleep—red like the wrappers. Way up above there was a muffled crackling like fists beating on a sheet of zinc, and a crescendo whine and a fresh fire flared up on the shore. The wind seemed torn the other way, and up from the very bed of the river came a trembling roar and both boats shuddered, buckled and shuddered again. On the downstream side of London Bridge another hissing whine brought back an even louder echo, a rushing roar culminating in a tearing, slithering sound of rubble falling from a height.

I was conscious of the blisters on my hands. The cans twinged my palms as though they were red-hot. Another fire-boat and three barges and then, in blurred silhouette against the new blaze, we saw the *Massey*. As we veered over towards her on our way down to Tower Bridge, her moniter was crackling like a stock-whip. A tall, ragged-topped wall, sullen-red, slowly, almost reluctantly, toppled landwards.

When dawn broke, the Thames was rising and more water was coming through the hard-won relays. The trickle of Home Counties support pumps also grew and began to relieve the exhausted London men who had faced seven hours of the most intense, difficult and frustrating fire-fighting in the history of the British fire service.

The 'all clear' sounded just before 6am, yet the St Paul's and Elephant fires and a hundred others were still not under control. Once water was available in greater quantities, barrages of cooling jets were set up to protect adjacent property and buildings at risk. Jackson's senior officers, from the City to the West End and from the Elephant to Shadwell, had long since accepted that the huge fires would need hundreds of men and a guaranteed supply of mains water to achieve complete control. On that morning, as the outlook brightened a little, it was still a case of first surrounding the larger fire zones and simultaneously protecting the immediate property, then squeezing the tired crews with their jets slowly in towards the centre of the fire, perhaps over a quarter of a mile wide. Even if the huge amounts of water needed could be relied upon, and likewise the courage and stamina of the fire-fighters, this was no easy task. Jackson's men could see that the bigger incidents would burn for many hours.

The firemen manning the branches, some perched high on ladders, others on roofs or on top of piles of unsteady brick-work, were to a man almost asleep on their feet. Few fire-fighters had been able to leave their posts for what refreshments were available during the raid. The 'all clear' must have been a delight for them to hear and the brightness of the dawn almost too harsh for their red-rimmed, bloodshot eyes. Some men were asleep in the streets, absolutely drained of strength and unable to stay awake any longer. Dewsbury Dessau recalled how sweet was the coming of the day: 'Nosing on the making tide towards Blackfriars I was suddenly conscious of the brittle lightness of things. A red blotch passed over the bridge above. It was a bus and meant morning . . .'

WORST FIRE RAID OF THE WAR

In the growing dawn the damage to the capital was overwhelming. Although the threat to St Paul's was receding, five of Wren's smaller City churches had been devastated. Both Westminster Hall and Westminster Abbey had lost their roofs and the debating chamber of the House of Commons was burnt out. Elsewhere, many other national buildings had suffered in the holocaust. In the City area these included the north wing of the Old Bailey and Gray's Inn Hall. Five livery halls had been reduced to piles of smoking, steaming and blackened ruins. Over thirty-five factories producing war equipment had also been hit during the raid: their products ranged from tank parts to flotation jackets for airmen.

Just before 7am, Jackson cancelled all officers' leave and ordered 1,000 relief firemen and 500 pumps from Home Office Control to be ready on the borders of London before darkness fell. It was imperative that the capital's fire defence should not fail.

A fleet of more than a hundred canteen vans attempted to get across London to provide food and hot drinks for the thousands of heroes of the night, but because of the great demands on the men, especially at the City and Elephant and Castle fires, many went hungry. Auxiliary Fireman Henry Stedman later wrote:

Of all my many fires I think that one was the worst. My feet ached so badly I could hardly stand, and I felt so tired and exhausted that when we were at last given a meal it required concentrated effort to eat it. All that I wanted was to sleep and to go on sleeping, but that was denied us. After about five hours we were called out again to pit our feeble powers against the holocaust that still raged in many places.

By mid-afternoon Jackson's officers reported that the City and Elephant and Castle conflagrations were coming under control and that St Paul's Cathedral and Faraday Building were out of danger. The single remaining large fire in the vaults of Waterloo Station was to burn for another four days before the LFS got the upper hand, finally attacking it at close quarters through the underground chambers via large holes cut in the hot platforms above the hidden inferno.

The thoughts of Jackson, Kerr, Fordham, Blackstone and other LFS senior officers were directed towards fighting the fires of yet another night of bombing. With hundreds of appliances, men and hose still committed to cooling down operations, how could the LFS face another onslaught from the Luftwaffe? Late that Sunday afternoon, the Metropolitan Water Board officially told the LFS headquarters that more than 1,000 acres of London around Shoreditch and London Bridge were entirely without water, and would remain that way for several days.

By the time night fell, the LFS could hardly be described as being prepared. The maximum number of pumps had been called back from damping down duties in preparation for a follow-up raid. Most AFS men waited for the first bombs and fire calls in their still soaking tunics. Not many could have felt that the LFS now had the measure of the Luftwaffe.

At RAF Fighter Command the plots showing the Channel and south-eastern England remained empty of enemy aircraft symbols; as the night slowly wore on, it became clear that there would not be a return raid. The 'all clear' earlier in the day had marked not only the end of the worst fire raid on London of the entire war, but of a change of enemy tactics. Within two weeks, the Luftwaffe Air Fleet Two, the force responsible for the regular bombing of London, had been moved to the Russian front. For the weary men and women of the LFS and the people of London, the blitz was at an end.

9

Aftermath

The statistics of the final air-raid of 10–11 May 1941 were staggering: Over 507 aircraft bombed London on that night and many of them returned to their home airfields, refuelled and reloaded with bombs, and came back for a second attack. The bomb tonnage dropped in the two sorties totalled 711 tons of high explosives (including parachute mines) and 86 tons of incendiaries.

700 acres of London were damaged by fire and 2,200 fires were recorded. The largest of these included: 9 conflagrations (fires burning out of control); 20 major fires (needing over thirty pumps); 37 serious fires (needing up to thirty pumps); 210 medium fires (needing up to ten pumps). Almost 1,500 people were killed during the raid; 1,800 badly injured; and 12,000 made homeless. But for the steady battle fought by the LFS, vast areas of the capital would have burned uncontrolled to become another Great Fire of London.

Jackson restored officers' leave forty-eight hours after the raid, by which time London had had two completely peaceful nights. LFS officers had been at work supervising fire-fighters non-stop since the evening of the raid, and although many firemen had worked well beyond their duty hours during that terrible night, most had been relieved by the incoming shift during the morning of 12 May. Numerous fires started by the raid continued to burn for days and the last LFS pump was not withdrawn until 22 May.

A typical blitz scene. Several crews of firemen attack a large warehouse fire. Two effective jets are at work although the crew manning the large radial branch in the centre are waiting for water. Note the firemen on far left who have turned their hose on to the face of unaffected premises to prevent fire spread by radiated heat. The facial expressions show the tension of the moment. Photograph taken by light from fire alone. Tabernacle Street, Shoreditch, EC. 11 January 1941 (*Daily Mirror*)

Canteen van scene with two AFS firewomen dispensing hot drinks. Note firemen's respirators worn in front mounted pack and neck curtain fitted to steel helmets to reduce effect of heat and falling sparks (*Daily Mirror*)

The last major fire raid. A six storey office block and warehouse blazes and very little water is available for fire-fighting. Elephant & Castle, South London. 10 May 1941 (*LFB*)

A towing van and trailer pump that have come to grief in a bomb crater. Southwark Bridge. 10 May 1941 (*LFB*)

FIRST STEPS TO A NATIONAL FIRE SERVICE

In the wake of this almost fatal blow to the capital, many senior fire officers were adamant that never again should London have to face such a risk, which was largely the result of inefficient mobilisation of back-up crews and appliances from other areas. All those who had experienced LFS convoys to the provinces had seen at first-hand the problems of the smaller brigades, and the unnecessary damage that had taken place through ineffective fire-fighting. In March there had been a collective approach to Major Jackson, who in turn suggested that they give an account of their convoy experiences to Eric Salmon, the clerk to the London County Council. This was done and the outcome was a meeting the following day when the officers met Sir George Gater, the secretary to the Ministry of Home Security. Also present at the meeting was Sir Arthur Dixon, then head of the fire service division of the Home Office, who asked the London officers for their solution to the problem. John Fordham, the veteran of Thameshaven, the Elephant and Castle and hundreds of other blitz fires, replied 'nationalisation'. He wanted one chain of command, standard uniforms, rank markings, conditions of service, training and equipment. But Dixon's verdict was clear: 'Nationalisation is impossible—the whole of history is against it.'

As the raids in the provinces continued and the damage soared, the groundswell of opinion in the fire service favouring nationalisation grew. During April, senior government members were lobbied and letters on the subject began to appear in *The Times* and *The Daily Telegraph*. Yet the attitudes of local authorities to the fire service were still amazingly varied—at worst, appalling. Some authorities had still not provided a towing vehicle for each pump, and incidents of firemen pulling pumps to blitz fires were not uncommon.

Ultimately, as a result of the deep-seated professional and public feeling on the subject, a report was placed before the

Home Secretary, Herbert Morrison. During a recent Question Time in the Commons, Morrison had been asked how many professional firemen had been recalled from active service. The Home Secretary had replied that in the previous twelve months more than 4,300 firemen recruited into the services had been released for home fire-fighting duties, and of these 482 were LFB men. Later on, Morrison had openly admitted that fire-fighting had become a 'military operation'.

On the evening of 18 April 1941, Herbert Morrison summoned Sir George Gater, Sir Arthur Dixon and Commander Firebrace to a conference at the Home Office. The meeting lasted four hours and went on until 2am; out of these discussions the National Fire Service was born. Morrison hurriedly consulted with local authorities about the government's plans for a unified service and only three days after the massive London raid of 10 May, he introduced the Fire Service (Emergency Provisions) Bill 1941 in the Commons. Within a week the bill had been through all the necessary stages and, on 22 May, received the royal assent. Through the new enabling powers and legislation, the secretaries of state could carry out the complete nationalisation of the British fire service.

The broad plan was to amalgamate all existing brigades in the United Kingdom into twelve regions, each being further sub-divided into fire forces. The government was to undertake the whole cost of the emergency services and pay a quarter of the normal annual cost of a professional fire brigade. There was also a promise given by the Home Secretary in the House of Commons, that the creation of the National Fire Service was an emergency wartime measure and that at the end of hostilities, the fire brigades would return to local authority control. London was to be Number Twelve Region and comprise numbers Thirty-Three to Thirty-Eight fire forces which collectively superseded the old LFB area, its AFS and the other sixty-six brigades in the region.

THE NFS IS BORN

On 18 August 1941, the NFS came into being. The fire service journal *Fire* recorded:

> Excluding the London region, Great Britain, for the purposes of fire defence, is now divided into thirty-nine fire force areas.
>
> Constitution of these fire forces is much on the lines advocated in *Fire* long before the first hostile act occurred, and only to be derided in bureaucratic circles!
>
> The unit is the division, comprised of two columns, ten companies, and twenty sections, with a total of one hundred pumps, that is five pumps to a section.
>
> There may be more than one division in each fire force, the latter of which will be under a fire force commander responsible to the regional commissioner and the senior regional fire-officer.
>
> The fire force commander will have wide powers. He will be empowered to transfer full-time officers and men from district to district within his area of command, but, says the Home Office, the number of such transfers must be kept as low as possible and must be in accord with local requirements.

Herbert Morrison himself issued the first orders of the day on 18 August to the National Fire Service:

> I am proud to be the first to address you by this title.
>
> On this day the National Fire Service comes into being and you who have been members of the fire brigades maintained by local authorities and members of the Auxiliary Fire Service, men and women, whole-time and part-time, take your places in the ranks of the nation's unified fire service.
>
> You stand in the front rank of our defence against the menace of air attack. You have faced tasks such as no fire brigades in the world's history have ever been called upon to perform. Bravely and with devotion you have done your duty. I am glad to bear this tribute to the work of the local authorities and their fire services.
>
> Now you step forward into a new service planned to meet grave tasks that lie ahead. The present change is being made in order to weld the many local fire services into a single national service, which can be more effectively organised, trained and directed for large-scale fire-fighting operations.

You will bring into the new service a fine spirit of courage and co-operation. See that it is used to the full, in the wider organisation of the National Fire Service, to which you now belong. I look to you to carry the fire service to new levels of achievement.

In the name of the nation whom you have served and will serve so well, I thank you for what you have done, and I charge you: Train, Organise, Practise and Be Ready.

As far as the LFS was concerned, there was little immediate change. In fact, the London fire-fighters were as a large unit already more experienced, more organised and better equipped than anywhere else in Great Britain. Because of this, the LFS had been much better able to withstand the battering of the blitz than had the provincial cities. After all, the LFS possessed one-third of the country's fire-fighting capacity.

Many LFS officers were appointed to senior positions in the NFS and Commander Firebrace was made chief of staff at the Home Office. Major Jackson remained in charge of the London region with the appointment of chief commander. As the NFS organisation got under way, many of the London blitz veterans had little good to say of it. The move towards nationalisation had coincided with the end of the big raids and some firemen resented the new set-up and blamed it for the continuing lack of action. During the earlier nightly raids and right up until 10 May 1941, many routine orders and station procedures had been waived. As things began to tighten up once more there was a feeling that the NFS was bringing about an unnecessary discipline. An ex-London AFS fireman recalled: 'We did all right in the blitzes without all that new bullshit—why should we have to put up with it after?'

NEW TECHNIQUES AND DEVELOPMENTS: 1941–4

Even if that was a commonly held view on the lower decks of the London region, the NFS was making great strides in the important field of training. The service generally had no standard handbook dealing with their profession of fire-fighting and for both recruits and aspiring junior officers, the whole process of training was a rather hit-and-miss affair. Under the aegis of the Home Office, the first collective volumes of the *Manuals of Firemanship* began to be prepared. When published in 1942, they totalled seven volumes and numbered over 1,300 pages: these formed the theoretical basis that is still the foundation of fire service theory and practice today. Another important new publication was the NFS *Drill Book*. This laid down concise details for the handling of pumps and other equipment at drill sessions. Very soon, firemen from London could drill alongside, say, a crew from a Midland region and be au fait with each other's part in a given drill sequence, which was a dramatic progression for the fire service.

Standardisation of uniforms and rank markings was yet another late-1941 NFS achievement and saw the end of the ex-LFB peakless sailor-type cap, worn during fire-station work and instruction periods. It gave way to the shiny, peaked AFS issue that already was widely worn throughout the country.

Other than a small and localised air-raid over London on 28 July, the lull continued while the efforts of the Luftwaffe were concentrated on fronts remote from the capital. At fire stations, drills and exercises again became the order of the day; surprisingly quickly, the huge numbers of pumps and ancillary vehicles lost their original brigade legends to become just numbers in the NFS fleet. Still no raids came to test the efficiency and organisation of the new service, although few outside London doubted that any such attack would be better dealt with than in the past.

In London, between calls to ordinary fires, the fire stations were increasingly slack, although it was still normal practice to mobilise several pumps to each call. Only at the occasional fire were twenty or more pumps required and there were over 1,250 appliances ready at any one time in Inner London. Despite the many hours taken up by lectures, drilling, cleaning and testing gear, boredom and frustration grew. Having already gone through the demoralising lull of 1939–40, then experiencing the virtual non-stop action of the blitz, few men welcomed the renewed quiet spell.

During late 1941, an activity commenced in fire stations that did much to improve the sagging morale of London region personnel: a toy-making scheme. It was hugely successful, both in its initial stages, right through the remaining war years and beyond. During the blitz period and subsequent evacuation of children, many day-nurseries had been set up by the Ministry of Health and local authorities, and they were drastically short of toys. In the middle of the drive towards the war effort, there was clearly no labour or money for them. A voluntary committee was formed to look into the problem and the result was an approach to Major Jackson to see if any London firemen would be prepared to give up a little of their stand-down time to produce some 'scratch-built' toys.

From that point things moved rapidly. District organisers from the London NFS were elected and small funds were secured for paint and tools. Within several weeks of the first meeting some beautiful and well-constructed toys were pouring out of fire-station 'workshops' to nurseries throughout the country. The material used to make the toys was mainly the timber dumped in large quantities on various sites by local boroughs from blitzed properties. It included charred flooring, doors, staircases and damaged furniture, together with a small amount of industrial scrap. The service provided lorries to collect the timber needed and the men were allowed to use corner spaces and lofts at stations to set up the toy workshops, where much midnight oil was burnt. Even relatively unbending officers soon saw the morale value of the exercise, which they allowed 'subject to no lowering of operational efficiency'.

So successful was the scheme that it quickly spread to the provinces, permitting the several thousand London men involved to concentrate on the growing number of nurseries in the metropolis. A similar project was also initiated by the women of the London NFS, who made a large number of soft toys during the lull periods of watchroom and control-room duties. As if to set the seal on the whole idea, wherever possible London firemen and women were allowed to deliver their gifts to the nurseries personally; this undoubtedly proved to be the most satisfying aspect of the whole operation.

THE CHRISTMAS PARTY AND OTHER DIVERSIONS

The first Christmas enjoyed by the NFS was a quiet one. The festive season of 1940 had come amid big raids, but a year later the direction of the war had, if only temporarily, moved away from the fire service. Stephen Spender joined the 34th fire force of the London region of the NFS in September 1941 and recalled his first Christmas spent on duty as a fireman. He was stationed at an outer London station where 'the brass of the fire-fighting appliances had to be polished every day; in central London it is painted over'.

The station consists of three army huts. One of these huts is a dormitory, another is kitchen and messing-room, another is known as the recreation-room. There are usually twenty to twenty-five men on duty, and seventeen of them are to be found, at any time after one o'clock in the afternoon, sitting in the recreation-room, playing cards, listening to the wireless, playing billiards or darts and even doing carpentry. All these activities go on at once, and a good deal of shouting as well.

The station has all the characteristics of a single group mind rather than a collection of individual minds. In many ways it is like a family, perhaps because we live all in one room together. Perhaps also Jimmy, the station officer, makes it a family by being so obviously a father figure. Jimmy is aged sixty-five and should have retired just about when the war began. He has been an ordinary fireman all his life. Instead of being retired, though, he has been promoted to sub-officer and put in charge of a station. He has white hair and a flabby face with eyes full of a kind yet jittery expression. These eyes pop out of creased lids and sockets which have the texture, and are about the size of, oyster shells. His eyes look like poached eggs served up in oyster shells. Their expression is due to the war between his natural inclination to be an inferior, and a desperate need to assert himself and keep his position. He is terrified of losing his pension . . .

The old hands do not altogether trust Jimmy. They say that he is two-faced and will do nasty things behind your back. He certainly can, out of sheer downright misery, turn nasty sometimes. However, the worst crime they ever suggested he might commit was to put down the bells during the night or when we were having supper. 'That's just the sort of thing that old sod would do,' they said, with voices full of bitter disillusion . . .

The Christmas party took about a month to prepare. These preparations caused some inconvenience as they meant our being turned out of the recreation-room, in the later stages of the decorating. The decoration of this room was the only example I have seen in practice of what you might call English Folk Art. The result shows how little modernism, surrealism and abstract ideas of art have reached the life of the people. English tolerance consists of letting intellectual movements glide over it as water over a duck's back. Left to themselves the firemen of the station did as follows:

First of all they blocked up all the windows of the already dark and fairly airless recreation-hut. Then they procured reams of crinkly paper—some of it a dark olive-green colour, the rest a light blue—and yards of paper ribboning. They covered the walls with the dark green paper, except for the window spaces, which they covered with the blue. Then they made a lattice-work of paper ribboning on the green part of the walls by drawing the ribbons, twisted, diagonally across the wall from floor to ceiling, cross-wise. Then they filled the blue spaces of the windows with a silver crescent moon and a few stars. In front of this they superimposed curtains of yellow tissue paper.

There were the usual streamers and festoons of coloured paper, right across the room, of course. Next, they moved the stove, which was by the door, right to the back end of the room, and they painted it all over with bright silver paint. Then they built a bar by the door where the stove had been. The front of this was also festooned with trellis-work of paper ribbons. Next, they procured hundreds of little 'fairy' bulbs which were hidden amongst the paper festoons suspended from the ceiling . . .

The Christmas party started at three o'clock in the afternoon, after a large Christmas lunch. Relatives began to float in, and some of them went away long before the actual dancing began, which was not 'til about seven. They had come simply to 'see the decorations', in the spirit in which one visits an art exhibition; and in a way it was an art exhibition. They were certainly not disappointed by the dazzling spectacle, illuminated by all its glittering lights, and with the silver stove shining like a mirror, in the recreation-room.

The party began very slowly. Most of the guests sat in rows on the chairs on either side of the room, waiting to be introduced to each other and then not knowing what to do when they were. What they were really waiting for was someone to be 'the life and soul' of the party. Convention demands this. While they waited, they ate a lot of mince pies, sandwiches and trifle. By about ten o'clock things had warmed up owing to the efforts of Joe, who led a dance in which everyone trooped single file in procession round the room. Then two or three of the guests sang sentimental songs. For these, the room was plunged into darkness, and the spotlight was directed on the singer's face.

At this point there was some competition between Spotty and Buzz, the most exhibitionistic men in the station, as to which of them should sing . . .

The party ended (officially) with speeches from Jimmy, and the leading firemen. Jimmy's speech began: 'I've got a fine lot of boys, a finer lot you won't see nowhere. I'm proud of them: honest I am.' At this point he was interrupted by a deafening roar of: 'Tell us the old, old story.'

Weissmann and Hertzberg made tactful little speeches. They were followed by one from an officious leading fireman with a little toothbrush moustache, like Hitler's. He said: 'Tonight we've enjoyed ourselves, boys. Well, tomorrow we'll get on with the Job.' There followed a great deal more about the Job.

This seemed extraordinary to me, as the Job consisted, usually, of scrubbing the station in the morning, and then hanging about for the rest of the day. However, it hypnotized the others. 'The Job, the Job!' cried Spotty, and he got up, and himself made an eloquent speech: 'We've all had a bloody good time tonight, boys. Tomorrow we get on with the Job.'

After this I had to go to the watchroom, which was simply part of the same recreation-room, separated by a thin partition. Through the walls I could hear Spotty and Buzz quarrelling as to who should sing a final song.

I must have been rather drunk, because next morning I discovered that I had written into the Occurrence Book at midnight: 'Fireman Spender in the watchroom', followed immediately by 'Fireman Spender on patrol', an impossible division of duties. I felt strangely ashamed of attributing so much activity to myself. It would have been nicer if I had left my own name out, and written down the names of all of them.

Another scheme was introduced in 1942 which allowed London firemen and women to participate in wartime industrial production by taking on a variety of assembly, finishing and testing work which required little space and simple tools. Small 'factories' were set up at many fire stations and over the months of 1942–3 millions of items as diverse as wireless sets, radar components, engine parts, mine fuses, stirrup pumps and bomb saddles all came off the production lines at London fire stations. After a 5 per cent deduction for NFS overheads and a large element paid to the Treasury, the balance was devoted to the improvement of general welfare and recreational facilities throughout the London region. Still, there were few suitable materials and goods available for the purpose and much of the quarter-of-a-million pounds raised was donated to charities, including the old LFS Benevolent Fund.

At fire stations with sufficient space, firemen were keeping chickens, pigs and goats. Many stations were also self-sufficient in vegetables and fruit. In the summer a number of crews were dispatched into the Home Counties to assist with hay-making, fruit-picking and harvesting, while remaining ready to respond to serious fires in London or in the area in which they found themselves. It was a useful arrangement, giving the firemen a chance to get away from the capital, albeit a hard-working one, and extremely valuable for the farmers who were hard-pressed for labour.

THE RAIDS OF 1942–3

During 1942–3, there were only twenty-eight air-raids over London, each consisting of the old mixture of high-explosive and incendiary bombs. In both the number of enemy aircraft involved and damage caused, these raids were minimal compared to those of 1940–1. The fires caused totalled 225— a far cry from the 2,000 calls per night in the blitz. They gave little opportunity for the NFS organisation to be tested under the sort of operational conditions that the LFS had faced night after night earlier in the war. Many incendiaries were in fact being dealt with initially by fire watchers, now far more experienced than previously.

The London region still found that they were called upon to support neighbouring regions, beginning in April 1942, for the three-month period of the 'Baedeker' fire raids. Hitler had said he would raze every British town listed in the Baedeker guidebook to Britain, which detailed the towns of special historic importance.

In April and May, London convoys travelled to Norwich, Reading, Exeter, Bristol, Bath, Oxford and Taunton, either to participate in fire-fighting or provide local fire cover for a depleted area. In June and early July, the raiders struck at Canterbury and Norwich (several times), and there were also London moves to cover raids in Weston-super-Mare, Peterborough and Birmingham. Generally, the whole process of convoy reinforcement was functioning more smoothly, without the problems of the past.

NFS PAY AND TRAINING

In its first year, the NFS establishment grew considerably and via the National Service Act, men and women were duly directed into the fire service. But there were anomalies. Not a few men who had been serving as part-time firemen before call-up, and who would have been excellent material for the NFS, found themselves drafted to other sections of the services. And, of course, there were those made to join the NFS against their wishes. Even so, by the spring of 1942, the London region establishment of the NFS stood at over 42,000 men and women.

Before the formation of the NFS many brigades, including London, had formed their own benevolent funds for the widows and families of firemen killed during the blitz. There was also an obvious need for some form of financial support for firemen invalided out of the service, often with little or no compensation from public funds. Over the months of raiding, these funds had grown considerably, frequently supplemented by donations, large and small, from members of the public. Under the NFS, the various funds were amalgamated, and the NFS Benevolent Fund was born.

Another early result of nationalisation was clear recognition by the government that if fire-fighters were to be effective the supply of water must be as protected as possible. Accordingly, £4 million of government aid was allocated during 1942 to the NFS for the provision of more satisfactory water supplies. Bore-hole pumps were installed on river barges and wharves; these were immersed pumps capable of delivering 2,000gpm at street level, irrespective of the state of the Thames. Over 1,000 miles of 6in steel piping was delivered, much of it to the London region, and greater emphasis was placed during training periods on the fast laying of this valuable portable pipeline.

In January 1943, Major Jackson resigned his post as chief commander NFS London region to take up a position as fire protection adviser in the Department of Scientific and Industrial research. It was a sudden resignation which saddened the personnel of the London region, particularly Jackson's old LFB men. He had valiantly led and guided the LFS through all the traumas of the pre-blitz lull and the subsequent action. However, he had grown increasingly irritated by interference from the civilian deputy regional commissioner in operational matters. F. W. Delve, CBE, former chief officer of the Croydon Brigade and Deputy Chief Inspector of Fire Service, was appointed Chief Regional Fire Officer of London in Jackson's place.

The rate of pay for an NFS fireman was increased to £3 10s per week, which brought it into line with the Civil Defence rate. Many men in the service had special skills, as motor mechanics, fitters, bricklayers and plumbers, etc, and these were used to the full. After consultation with the appropriate trade unions, rates of pay were agreed which allowed the NFS to use the skills: there was a tremendous backlog of maintenance and repairs to the thousands of pumps and other appliances. Similarly, building work on fire stations had been neglected during the blitz and new projects remained unfinished.

During the enforced lull of 1943–4, the River Thames formation of the London region of the NFS undertook a considerable programme of training firemen from other regions who were destined to be posted to fireboat service. Harold Harvey, who had joined the AFS in Derby earlier in the war, was one sent to Lambeth on a month's attachment to the River Thames section. Under the watchful eye of the London instructors, his group underwent an intensive course on fireboat pumps and equipment, knots and lines, laying hose lines ashore, boat handling and, least enjoyed, rowing! Most 'hose ashore' was done by fireboat crews working from skiffs. Harvey recalled hours of rowing in full uniform under a hot June sun with, at times, an eight-knot tide running. Occasionally, to the crew's delight, the London instructor at the tiller relented and suddenly steered alongside a Thameside flight of steps, at the top of which was an inviting tea-shop or stall.

Another interesting deployment for London firemen during the lull on the home front was a concentrated effort at the construction sites of Mulberry Harbour caissons on the banks of the Thames. When a completed caisson was ready for launching, it was necessary to remove tons of soft mud from the construction basin in order to float the 40ft high structure from the site. A total of 400 firemen were engaged for six months on this task, clearing the mud by using their high-powered water jets. Teams of men worked continuously through the bitterly cold winter months of 1943–4, frequently spending hours standing thigh-deep in the mire.

PREPARING FOR D-DAY

As the build-up in preparation for the Allied invasion of Europe grew, large quantities of ammunition, vehicles and valuable stores were being assembled along the South Coast. To provide additional fire cover for these areas, especially to guard against enemy air-raids upon such strategic targets, sixty London region pumps were sent south to supplement a number of appliances already in position from northern NFS regions. Before D-Day, this force numbered some 10,000 men and 2,000 women.

A specialised force set up by the NFS at that time was an 'overseas contingent', formed entirely of volunteers who underwent a rigorous, specialised training. Their purpose was to give fire cover in the vicinity of the Normandy landings, for huge amounts of supplies would flood in once the invasion started. They were also to be on hand with their pumps if the Germans retreated under a 'scorched earth' policy. From the start there were problems of who would have ultimate command of the NFS columns; it seemed the military preferred to use their own well-trained but small units of the Army

Fire Service. In the event, the NFS contingent was ignored after the D-Day landings, and it was not until October 1944 that Herbert Morrison announced that the War Office had decided to disband the NFS overseas columns and return all personnel to their home units. Despite this, the United States Army requested the use of one of the fire-fighting columns. In January 1945, the column embarked for France where they performed their duties admirably, serving beside American troops across Europe and into Germany.

1944 opened with a series of raids that became known as 'the Little Blitz'. It started with two very light raids on the nights of 3 and 14 January; but on the night of 21 January the enemy returned to attack in earnest with a raid which, although not to be compared with those of 1940–1, was more intense than any experienced in the intervening period. Arrangements had already been made to cope with this anticipated development in the enemy's tactics, for during the last months of 1943 it had been apparent that the Allied preparation for the invasion of the Continent would become a target for the Luftwaffe and again fire was likely to be the main weapon. With this in mind, the winter had been spent in developing a more effective fire-watching scheme. A re-organisation also took place in the London region to make sure that appliances were quickly on the spot to deal with fires resulting from the new German technique of dropping very heavy, close concentrations of incendiary bombs. The raid on 21 January followed just that pattern and the fire service plan to cope with such a situation proved successful.

Raids employing the new method of concentrated incendiary-bomb attack were repeated on seven occasions in February, four in March and two in April, and at one time seemed likely to reproduce on a minor scale the events of 1940–1. Fortunately the efficiency of the fire service response was such that on no occasion did the situation give cause for alarm and no further raids on London by piloted aircraft were experienced after 19 April 1944.

The larger numbers of men in the service made possible a long-overdue reduction in the duty system. In November, the fireman's working week was shortened to eighty-four hours, which meant being on duty for twenty-four hours and then off duty for the following twenty-four.

In a parliamentary sense, 1944 closed on a historic note for the NFS. In June, the Home Office had suddenly realised that the regulations which had brought about nationalisation three years before had not been placed before parliament. Theoretically, the NFS was illegal! No legislator, parliamentarian, government official or fire-service officer had realised the default. Within days, Herbert Morrison had apologised to the House of Commons and an indemnity bill was passed, although this didn't prevent rumblings about 'the dangers of delegated legislation'!

The morning after the last major fire raid. A view looking north from the dome of St Paul's soon after daylight with a wide area of damage visible and many fires still burning. The Old Bailey stands proudly above the smoke, although it has itself suffered some damage. 11 May 1941 (*LFB*)

The new weapon arrives. The scene soon after a VI flying bomb has fallen with firemen, civil defence and police beginning search and rescue operations. Middlesex Street, E1. 10 November 1944 (*LFB*)

The wider devastation caused by the V2 rockets. Part of a whole street has vanished under tons of rubble. Mackenzie Road, Islington, North London. 20 December 1944 (*LFB*)

There were amazing escapes. This woman survived this V1 attack. Whitta Road, Manor Park, East London, late 1944 (*LFB*)

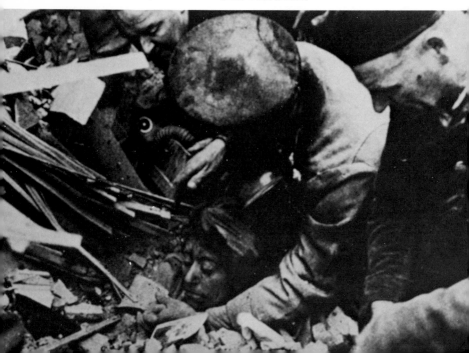

10

The New Menace: a Daily Horror

Contrary to all expectations, the Allied assault on D-Day brought no enemy retaliatory bombing of embarkation points, docks or communications. However, the final phase of the war on the home front was not long in starting.

On 13 June 1944, at 3.50am, an alert sounded in the London area. Searchlights quickly had a plane in their silvery beams and intense anti-aircraft gunfire followed. Four minutes later, the NFS received a call to a crashed aircraft on open ground at Barking. The plane appeared to be an enemy aircraft and there was what was termed a 'small fire'. A leading fireman was burned about the face and hands during its extinction and at 4.05am, the 'all clear' sounded.

Little more than ten minutes later, the sirens were wailing again. The guns joined in and the din of their barrage rose to a crescendo, then suddenly ceased. Afterwards, a NFS officer described what happened:

> But instead of the expected quiet which usually follows, a loud sound was heard which I attributed to a single engined plane in a power dive. The sound of the engine continued for what I thought would be an extraordinarily long dive and as my thoughts flashed to a plane that might have been hit or which was in trouble, the engine sound ceased abruptly. There was silence for a few seconds, followed by a violent explosion which shook the whole neighbourhood.

The observation post attached to this officer's station at once called down, 'plane believed crashed about half a mile away', and gave bearings. When the officer drove out in the grey light of dawn to investigate, he found his way barred by a

dense cloud of dust and smoke. Underfoot there was glass
and rubble. He spoke to a warden who said that it was a high-
explosive bomb or something. There was considerable
damage and a railway bridge was down as well as houses
flattened. People were groaning and crying out. The NFS
officer called for more pumps and crews; within a few minutes
firemen were assisting bewildered and injured victims from
the devastation, working alongside all the other services
which had speedily appeared on the scene.

WHAT WAS IT?

What had really come down? That was the question being
debated right and left amongst all the services employed at
the 'incident'. Many said emphatically that it had been a
plane; but no bodies of airmen were recovered and no nuts
or bolts or parts commonly seen at an aeroplane crash were
found. A senior NFS officer reported half an hour after the
fall of the 'thing' that: 'Further pieces of metal have been
found which point to the possibility of a propelled projectile.'
The BBC and the London evening papers declared that two
planes had been brought down during the night.

The following Tuesday and Wednesday nights passed
quietly without incident, but at twenty-five minutes before
midnight on Thursday, 15 June, the alert sounded and the
guns went into action. Firemen in their observation post at
New Cross saw out of the barrage a flaming object diving to
the ground. A Jerry had copped a packet! They cheered as it
crashed and New Cross firemen turned out to the scene of
the impact. When they got there, there was no more cheering
that night. The chaos and damage wrought by the fallen
'aircraft' were shocking.

All through that short summer night, the din of the anti-
aircraft guns continued, and when daylight came it made no
difference. Amid the barrage there were tremendous intermittent explosions. The earth shook and soon after the fire-

bells rang as the service responded. Forty-four times that
night the NFS in London turned out to 'incidents', and in
nearly every case this was upon information received from
their own observation posts. On thirteen of these occasions
fire developed. The report issued by the regional fire mobilising officer the next morning read:

The enemy is reported to be using pilotless aircraft which
appear to cause extensive demolition and blast damage but
do not seem to possess exceptional incendiary qualities. The
incidence of the attack has been mainly in a wedge shape with
base at south-east quarter of circumference of London region
and apex in the centre.

This explanation solved the mystery of the plane crash in the
East End on the previous Tuesday. The VI had arrived.
Hitler's new weapon was a petrol-injection ram-jet flying
bomb, carrying 1,000kg of high explosive at a speed of 350
mph. The engines of these VIs would cut out shortly before
the projectiles fell and exploded on impact with the ground.

The 'all clear' sounded at 9.23am on Friday morning
after an alert that had lasted for more than nine hours. But the
respite from the gunfire and bombardment lasted only a few
minutes. In the control room at regional fire headquarters,
Lambeth, the red lamps lit up on the air-raid warning map
of London at 9.46am. One after another, messages came
through from the observation posts and VI incident after
incident was plotted on the wall map as the morning wore on.

'There was a time when he'd skulk off when it was getting
near daylight,' said one fireman, 'but it doesn't matter now.
All the Spitfires in the world can't put the breeze up a blinking
plane without a pilot.' It was true. Day or night now made no
difference to aerial attack. On that first day of bombardment,
further alerts sounded at 1pm, 2pm and at 9.25pm. Because
of the proven value of the observation posts, an NFS London
region order went out that they must be manned continually,
whether an alert had sounded or not.

FIRE AND CASUALTIES

The fall of Hitler's first V1 flying bomb ushered in the period of heaviest activity for the NFS in London. Firemen attended every incident and dealt with many fires resulting from the explosion of these missiles. Fire did not always follow, and on such occasions fire service personnel, appliances and equipment were used to augment the rescue and ambulance services in coping with the large number of casualties resulting from the widespread blast effect. The 'terror bombs' damaged buildings over a wide area and NFS resources were fully stretched in making 'first-aid' repairs to bomb-damaged houses, sheeting roofs to make buildings weatherproof, and in salvaging furniture and personal belongings from homes too severely damaged to be easily made habitable. These services kept any available firemen continually occupied, and did much to sustain London during a time of great ordeal. The service also helped in the renewed evacuation of women and children to safe areas in the country, and spent a good deal of time clearing up the shattered buildings of public services, particularly hospitals, enabling them to remain in operation.

Massed V1 attacks were experienced from June 1944 onwards, with a total of 638 flying bombs in that month alone. This meant an average of 12 per day during an attack, the peak days of which were 16 and 18 June. 1,121 V1s fell in July, and although the daily average then stood at 36, there were peak days: on 2 July 80 bombs fell, on 6 July 60; 22 July had 66; 28 July had 57. This was in spite of an average of 30 bombs a day being brought down by RAF fighters.

Some caused huge fires. On a cloudy morning in July, a V1 fell on a candleworks by the Thames. 'It was a building,' as the matter-of-fact fire report stated, 'of 300ft by 200ft, the contents of which were barrels and tanks of paraffin wax, 60 tons of fuel oil and 200 gallons of turpentine. There were barges containing paraffin wax moored alongside the factory.'

It was a fire-raiser's heaven. When the NFS arrived minutes after the explosion, they found a quarter of the building demolished and alight. An attempt was made to use foam to smother the fire, but this method normally relies for its effect upon the foam floating over the surface of the burning oil and cutting off the available oxygen. Because of the demolition, and the heaps of rubble, the foam did not seal off the flames as was hoped. Water was soon resorted to.

There was a constant danger of collapsing walls and roofs, while the fire-fighters groped through dense smoke and worked knee-deep in oil and molten wax which all the time threatened to ignite from burning wreckage. This did indeed happen. Within a single minute the fire had leapt over sheds, laboratory, quayside and barges. 'It was a miracle,' said one officer, 'that no firemen were trapped. We saw the flames suddenly roar up and rush towards us. We had to move.'

Having eventually deployed twenty-five pumps and five fireboats, the officer-in-charge of the fire reported two hours after the fall of the bomb: 'Fire well surrounded. No further help required.' However, it was another two hours before the last flame flickered and finally went out.

Another V1 flying bomb hit a Kennington gasometer. It penetrated the gas pipework and exploded in the retort house, setting fire to another gasometer and a 10,000 gallon paraffin holder, which fortunately was not full. The fire in the pipework was extinguished with two jets, while the only thing to do with the burning gasometer was to play six cooling jets on to its stanchions. Holes had been made in its side by fragments of bombs, but these were plugged with a quantity of clay. It was splendid improvisation on the part of the firemen who used dustbin lids and planks in the sealing operation. Nearby was a benzole plant and the meter house, and a water curtain was put up by using several jets thus saving the benzole plant from becoming involved, though the meter house suffered some damage.

For sheer volume of smoke, no fire at any other incident

equalled that at a tar installation when a flying bomb fell among the tar containers. Here the firemen had to work against a river of flowing burning tar. It went down the street like creeping lava from a volcano and a string of firemen dumped sacks of sand in its path in an attempt to check its course.

The most difficult rescue problems occurred when a fire was located deep down in an impacted pile of debris. A person trapped on an upper floor by fire was a relatively simple situation in contrast with one trapped beneath burning wreckage. Fire service and rescue officers were presented with appalling problems at flying-bomb incidents.

A bus garage at Elmers End was hit and in it were fifty-three buses. It also contained underground oil and petrol tanks and fifty cases of Home Guard ammunition. Fire was gaining a rapid hold and it was reported to NFS crews that a number of people were trapped beneath the debris between the canteen and some offices. Before the fire could be properly attacked, these people had to be rescued. When the fire-fighters were able to concentrate on the fire, the wreckage of buses and explosions from petrol tanks hampered operations. The buses had been garaged so closely together that they made narrow corridors of fire down which it was imperative that firemen ran their hoses. Eventually, the oil tanks and the ammunition were isolated. In the meantime, some of the buses were driven or rolled out of the garage; others burned with great intensity, their tyres appearing to catch alight at the outset with the sump castings burning fiercely because of their magnesium-alloy content.

It was at small fires in homes that problems of rescue were especially acute. In putting water on to hot debris there was always the likelihood of it coagulating and forming an almost impenetrable crust over anyone who might be trapped beneath it. The fires were often caused by a fractured gas pipe igniting, so that a victim was faced by the additional danger of being gassed. A fire officer who had attended an incident in which an elderly woman was affected in this way wrote afterwards:

> This is another case of rescue work being hampered by a gas pipe alight and so situated that to keep the fire down we chanced drowning the person; if we leave the fire the person may be burned to death; if we knock the fire out we risk gassing the person and rescuers. Turning the gas and water off during an alert would save us from making a decision which, in any case, generally means a life has to be lost.

Inevitably, because they were often the first organised helpers to arrive on the scene, firemen would encounter the 'walking casualties', and those dazed people seeking a way out of the chaos of demolition and the pall of dust and smoke. They would be the first to hear cries for help from the trapped victims, and if there was no fire present they were able to begin the task of rescue. By the time the VI arrived, most firemen in the London region had already undergone basic training in light rescue work and were able quickly to supplement the arduous work of the Civil Defence heavy gangs.

After one of the first VI incidents, in the much-bombed borough of Wandsworth, a column officer reported:

> We were there within two minutes of the bomb falling. I had all the appliances so deployed that the light from their head-lamps flooded the demolished houses, and for three-quarters of an hour the men worked digging out, carrying down and generally disposing the injured in positions as comfortable as possible, until the ambulances were available to fetch them. We laid them on our scaling ladders, or blown-off doors, on seats taken from cars and put them in towing vehicles or improvised shelters, for it was raining hard. The homeless but uninjured sat in other towing vehicles until they could be directed to rest centres. Our fellows went on doing first aid in the harsh glare of the headlamps.

Probably nothing could have been better for the morale of the people being subjected to such bombing, than the immediate presence of a uniformed and disciplined body of men. One of the first NFS crews would bring a first-aid box and every fireman had strong arms and cheering words. The Wandsworth column officer continued:

> We came upon an Anderson shelter that had been collapsed like a shut concertina. The crews got hold of the edges of the thing and tore it open. In cold blood they couldn't have done it, I'm sure. It was just the amazing strength that an emergency will give you.

Off Lewisham Market, where a bomb had come down without an alert sounding, a section-leader said: 'It was like an invasion beach. Best to forget it.'

'At one place,' said a fireman, 'we had to use saucepans and tin baths to pick up the remains. I've never seen such sights, either on battlefields or during the worst of the previous blitzes.'

For the firemen it was a test of nerve and stomach to work amid groans, cries of pain and in the presence of mutilated bodies and limbs. 'Some of the newer men had never seen a dead body before the flys came,' said a divisional officer. 'Yet now they'd do anything, although we use gloves sometimes, but it's not true that you get used to this rescue work at these incidents. It's a new set of people every time ...'

This part of the firemen's work was recognised by Chief Regional Fire Officer Delve, when he singled out certain actions and commended individuals. His bold commendations convey vivid pictures of the fire service at V1 incidents:

> 'While Section-Leader Briggs was attending a flying-bomb incident on 1 July 1944, at Colindale Hospital, Hendon, at about 0445 hours, oral contact was made with a woman trapped beneath a large quantity of debris. A very difficult situation developed. The personnel were working in a cavity, the roof of which consisted of debris supported by a 12ft by 6in rolled steel joist, which, in turn, was leaning against a damaged wall held in position by its own weight. A false move would have brought the whole of this down on the rescue party and trapped person. The woman was finally extricated without physical

injury and this operation was successfully completed only as the result of the work and initiative displayed by Section-Leader Briggs during the initial stages of the rescue. His calm, un-hurried efficiency did much to subdue the excitement and tendency to hurry which some of the personnel at the incident displayed.'

'Company Officer Dew forced an entry into a basement where he found two women. He enlarged the hole to enable a doctor to join him and it was then found that one woman was dead and would have to be moved to free the other woman. With the help of the Heavy Rescue Service the second woman was rescued alive. Company Officer Dew was in the basement for nearly two hours with a quantity of debris above him and his good work did much towards saving the woman from asphyxiation.'

'The crews were ordered to assist in extrication of casualties from demolished houses in West Park Avenue. After a careful survey casualties were believed to be trapped in number forty-six and their existence was confirmed by hearing a woman's voice calling for help. Firemen Carroll and Sturt began tunnelling. The first floor of the house had collapsed so that one end was resting on the ground floor and the other end was a few feet higher. Both firemen tunnelled in a prone position between the ground and first floor, passing out the debris to personnel outside. After cutting through furniture and brickwork, Carroll could hear the woman's voice im-mediately above his head. He inserted his arm through a cavity and it fell on the woman's face. She clasped his hand and asked for air. He reassured her and Sturt crawled out to obtain oxygen. By means of a length of a stirrup pump tubing, the oxygen was passed through to her from cylinders carried on the fire appliance. Fireman Sturt then decided to try to extricate the casualty by cutting a hole in the roof and gently working down to her. This, with the aid of men of the Heavy Rescue Service, he was able to do. She was finally rescued after two hours, during an hour and a half of which oxygen was supplied, four cylinders being used.'

A baker who had lost his shop at Crayford wrote: 'I would like to put on record my admiration of the fireman who res-cued my manageress alive and immediately after this went down again to endeavour to rescue an elderly woman, who was in the shop at the time. The fireman succeeded but unfortunately she was dead. This fireman was in absolute danger for the whole of the four hours in which he was tunnelling.'

A firm at Millwall testified to: '. . . the courage and energy displayed by members of the NFS. Everybody was deeply impressed by the extraordinary speed with which they arrived at our premises and how marvellously your men executed the work of rescue and salvage.'

A family at Streatham recognised that in this rescue work, 'the fire service is keeping up its tradition and is as usual doing wonderful work. My mother, sister and I were buried under debris. We were rescued by firemen. We shall never forget not only the speed and efficiency with which they worked, but also their kindness. Their cheerfulness and the encouragement they gave us did much to alleviate the dreadful experience.'

Unfortunately, not all rescues meant lives were saved. Perhaps the most tragic frustrated rescue was undertaken by No 34 fire force in London. Four children had been playing together in the kitchen of their house when a flying bomb hit the house next door. Roof and walls collapsed. A section-leader, leading fireman and two firemen went to the rescue of the children and worked their way to the middle of the house:

'Through a hole in the dividing wall we could see the children in the back room,' said Section-Leader Croker afterwards. 'We shored up the collapsed roof and floor above us and took the wall down brick by brick until we could reach them. Each of the children was trapped independently; we used a hacksaw to free one of the little girls from a folding chair.'

The firemen worked for about three hours in a space about 3ft high until all four children were freed. Two were already dead and the others died later in hospital.

The 100ft turntable ladders with which the NFS was equipped were on many occasions used to bring down people from the fourth, fifth or sixth floors where the rocket or bomb had ripped away half the building. Occasionally the ladder was used as a crane and a badly injured casualty would be strapped to a short wooden ladder or stretcher and lowered by means of a rope running over the head of the ladder. But there was at least one operation involving a turntable ladder that was unsuccessful.

It was in Bermondsey at 3am. A bomb had ripped away the front of a block of flats, leaving exposed five sagging floors. From the fifth could be heard the groans of a man. Because the staircase had been destroyed the only way up was by turntable ladder; any attempt to get up another way would have brought the hanging floors crashing down. Because of the debris it was not possible to get the ladders as close into the building as was desirable, but the ladders were extended until the head projected above the fifth floor and the danger 'overload' signal showed at the ladders' base control. Nevertheless, a fireman went aloft into the darkness and found the area of wrecked floor where the injured man lay. In turn an NFS officer went up and considered the situation and finally the Heavy Rescue officer went up to satisfy himself. They were unanimous. One more ounce of weight on the floor would bring it, the casualty and the rescuers to the ground. Shoring up was the only course. By the time that each floor had been made safe, valuable time had been lost, and when the rescuers reached the man he was dead.

For most of the time the NFS worked alongside the Heavy Rescue squads, and usually under the instructions of rescue officers. From the beginning of the flying-bomb attacks it was realised by NFS officers and the Civil Defence authorities that fire service techniques would have to be modified. A tendency to dash into the dust and smoke had to be checked and the two basic principles of rescue work had to be applied: (a) reconnaissance and a careful methodical approach; (b) working in from the perimeter of the incident and taking away the 'easy' casualties first. There could be no smash-and-grab tactics: enthusiasm had to be curbed and crawling over the debris was forbidden until it was known whether anybody was beneath it.

V2 ROCKETS

In August, although the daily average of flying bombs had dropped to 19 and the total for the month was 531, the peak day of the whole flying-bomb period occurred on 3 August 1944, when 97 flying-bomb incidents were attended by the fire service in the London region. Nine incidents were recorded on 1 September, the last day of the sustained attack, and from then on flying bombs were experienced only spasmodically. However, the reduction in scale of these attacks after 1 September, coincided with the introduction by the enemy of the second 'V' weapon. The V2 rocket was more deadly and carried a warhead of one ton of high explosive. The first of these giant missiles landed on Chiswick during the afternoon of 9 September, and the violence of its explosion was heard and felt many miles away. Unlike the flying bomb which gave long warning of its approach, the first intimation of the arrival of a rocket was its tremendous explosion and blast.

From the beginning of September onwards, the rockets arrived consistently, working up from a monthly total of 15 that month and 25 in October, to a peak of 116 in February 1945, and 115 in March. Yet there were times when even amid the wreckage there was cause for a smile. At one incident, firemen were trying to persuade a woman down a ladder from the first floor. 'But I can't come down,' she said tearfully, 'Not until I find my teeth!' Another time, in a partially demolished house, firemen in the course of their search came upon the recumbent figure of a man in bed. They removed the scattering of plaster and had mentally recorded the man as being dead, when he sat up: 'Here! What's all this? What's going on here?' he demanded with all the petulance of one disturbed from sleep.

On another occasion, a dog was heard whining on a first floor. A fireman ran up a ladder and found the dog in a corner of a shattered room. Carefully, he lifted the dog and brought it down the ladder and set it on the ground. Immediately the dog made straight back for the ladder, scrambled up it and disappeared into the corner from which it had been rescued. At an incident where the front of a house had been torn away, firemen's torches lit up the ruins. From an exposed bedstead came an angry voice: 'Take your bloody lights away, I want to get dressed!'

After a V1 had fallen on Putney General Hospital, a fireman saw the half-buried head and shoulders of a woman. He called his crew over and they started carefully moving the debris. After half a hour of lifting masonry and beams, one fireman was able to touch the woman; she was quite cold and there was no obvious sign of life in her. They worked on and as they carefully removed the rubble from around her, it was discovered that she was naked. Another few minutes and she was freed: a life-size anatomical model made of rubber and plastic.

Fortunately, the most intense attacks by the flying bombs took place when the nights were short; but when rockets and bombs fell during the hours of darkness rescuers were frequently hampered in their work. The fire service had been prepared for working at night, being provided with searchlights, floodlights, acetylene and oil lamps which the ex-LFB emergency tenders carried, but the equipment was not sufficient for the many calls now made on it. A number of night-time incidents in different parts of the London region simultaneously required lights for rescue work, so many emergency lighting units were formed—a lorry or towing vehicle with all the lamps that could be found—ready at a moment's notice for action.

Another regular part of the work was salvage operations. When the war began, salvaging was generally left to the London Salvage Corps, but the experience of the blitz had shown that a larger body of skilled men in this particular field was needed. The training of NFS firemen was therefore undertaken by instructors from the London Salvage Corps and in the re-organisation all the salvage tenders and their crews were attached to home stations. Subsequently, when a call came in that a flying bomb had fallen, the salvage tender was part of the 'first attendance' on the scene.

Salvaging consisted not only of dragging goods and chattels out of the way of a spreading fire, but of covering machinery and furniture with tarpaulins to prevent damage by water or weather. Much of the water which had been poured on to a fire was directed back to drains so that the minimum of damage was caused. The effects of blast as well as fire greatly extended the use of salvage crews at flying-bomb and rocket incidents.

One of the major incidents in which salvage crews were involved was at Chambers Wharf, a riverside grain warehouse in Rotherhithe: 6 salvage tenders were required. The great amount of water used on the fire caused the loose grain, linseed and peanuts to slowly choke the drains. Two hundred and ten salvage sheets were laid out to protect valuable food stocks and 12 Homelite pumps (special pumps used for salvage work) were used for about fourteen days to pump away water that was collecting all the time and threatening the stocks of food.

'At Powis Street,' related one officer, 'my salvage crew were employed in sweeping up the broken glass and light rubble in the road so that traffic could pass along. They damped the dust at another incident with a diffuser nozzle so that the rescue workers could work more easily in what had been intolerably dusty conditions. They also went looking for hanging window frames and other dangerous objects hanging from the face of buildings which might crown someone should they fall. They helped shop-keepers to board up their windows and so protect their goods. At one grocer's shop, I remember, they removed the entire stock to a safe place.'

Collectively, the carnage and destruction brought to the London region by the VI and particularly the V2, was awful. With their greater explosive capacity, the V2 incidents often ran into a hundred or more fatalities. On 25 November 1944, one fell on a block of buildings in New Cross, South London, killing 268 men, women and children. Three months later, at the height of the V2 campaign, a direct hit on buildings at Smithfield in the City of London, left 233 dead and as many injured.

FINAL PHASE OF THE WAR

As the Allied invasion forces progressively overran the German launching sites during the early months of 1945, the numbers of VIs and V2s falling over the London area diminished, despite the fact that both weapons were being launched from sites in Holland and Germany itself. The V2 rockets could be fired from mobile pads, yet in the final reckoning their end came within twenty-four hours of the last VI base being captured. Late in the afternoon of 27 March 1945, the final V2 fell near Orpington in Kent and only hours later the engine of the last VI cut out and fell on Chislehurst, also in Kent. No more would the sinister rumbling of the 'doodlebugs' be heard across the region, and no more would people run for cover when the VI engines faltered and began their short, accelerating and deadly fall to earth.

For the NFS it signalled the final phase of the war over London and the South East. There would be no more dramatic witness of the falling missiles by older firemen high up in their observation posts at fire stations. No longer would they sight and quickly plot the fall of the bombs and rockets and dispatch the waiting appliances and crews below. No more would firemen dig and burrow into the debris for casualties, often having to take cover themselves as further flying bombs fell nearby.

A grand total of 2,381 VIs and 511 V2s fell on the London

region in the nine months from June 1944, and at almost 900 of these incidents fires were caused. In the London County Council area, over 30,000 houses were completely destroyed and $1\frac{1}{4}$ million more damaged. Of all the Greater London area, the County Borough of Croydon was the worst hit with 139 flying-bomb incidents alone. Wandsworth, Lewisham, Woolwich and Silvertown all suffered particularly badly under Hitler's terror weapons.

The V1 and V2 period was every bit as traumatic as the blitz had been for London's fire-fighters, but brighter times ahead were clearly heralded not only by the news from Europe, but also by that very British institution, the weather. It had been an especially hard winter and one of the coldest Christmases of the entire war. This had meant freezing and miserable hours toiling amongst the bricks and rubble that were once offices, factories and homes, as the flying bombs and rockets continued to fall. But the last days of the German weapons over London coincided with the hottest period in March for fifty years. With the whole surviving population of the scarred and battered capital, the men and women of the NFS looked forward eagerly to the end of the conflict that had touched every man, woman and child in the Greater London area.

11

Retrospect

When peace in Europe was finally announced on 8 May 1945, 327 men and women of the London region of the NFS had been killed in action and over 3,000 injured. Of the final total of 875 operational fire stations in the London area, 662 were damaged at some time or other during the years of the war by fire, bombing or blast. Including the flying-bomb and rocket incidents, over 50,000 emergency calls had been attended by London's firemen.

Throughout the war, the bravery of the men and women of the capital's fire-fighting forces was regularly recognised and an impressive number of gallantry awards were won. These included 1 George Cross (Fireman Errington) and 38 George Medals, one of which was awarded to Auxiliary Firewoman Tanner for her coolness and courage under intensive bombardment on the night of 20 September 1940, when she volunteered to drive a petrol van into a major central London fire zone to allow the many pumps at work to be refuelled. The regional senior fire officer also commended 152 members of the LFB, AFS and latterly, the NFS, for outstanding acts of bravery; 17 of these awards went to firewomen. Other wartime recognition for London firemen included the awards of 1 CBE, 3 OBES, 13 MBES and 118 BEMS plus 11 King's Police and Fire Service Medals for Distinguished Conduct.

When Japan surrendered in 1945, the NFS was already trying to gear itself to its peacetime role and the promised return of fire brigades to local-authority control. The national strength of the NFS had been reduced to 52,000 and by the end of 1945 was down to 31,000. Yet the government was slow in announcing its plans for the fire service of the post-war years; it maintained that there was still much for the nation's firemen to do. Large numbers of wartime pumps and other equipment had to be mothballed or sold off and miles of emergency pipelines needed dismantling, and as well a growing number of 'ordinary' fires and other calls for assistance had to be answered. Ex-AFS members who had held key positions in industry and commerce were allowed to leave the service, but most of those conscripted men who wanted to be demobbed quickly had to stay on until the spring of 1946. In the London region this eventually left a hard core of ex-regular firemen and those AFS personnel who had warmed to their fire-fighting experiences and wanted to make the fire service their career. There was, however, a surplus of officers, arising from the original wartime need to supervise 100,000 men, and re-assessment boards were convened to resolve the problem.

After some procrastination by the Labour government of Clement Attlee, the Fire Service Bill was finally presented to Parliament on 1 February 1947. A whole fire-fighting era was over. The NFS was transferred back to local authorities on 1 April 1948, and 147 fire brigades, many of them larger and now the responsibility of county councils and county boroughs, were established. The proud title of the London Fire Brigade, still the largest in the United Kingdom, re-emerged in the grey austerity of the post-war years, its protection area unchanged from that of 1939.

The reconstituted London Fire Brigade and the brigades of Hertfordshire, Essex, Kent, Surrey, Middlesex, Croydon and West and East Ham went forth into their new role, their personnel having experienced at first-hand months of fire-fighting of the most physical nature. At the height of the raids, the wartime fire-fighters had been bombed, strafed, burnt, scorched and frozen, almost suffocated by smoke, and had run the risk of being crushed by falling walls and masonry.

Never had the fire service of London been found wanting in its response.

In attempting to describe what fire-fighting is really like at close hand, one rapidly runs out of suitably crisp phraseology. From the standpoint of forty years' progress into the technology of today's fire-fighting equipment, it is easy to forget that at the height of the blitz London's firemen had little breathing apparatus at their disposal and pitifully poor communications. In fact, radio was not available to the fire service until the war was almost over; during many of the worst air-raids, especially the City raid of 29 December 1940 and the far wider raid of 10 May 1941, firemen were trying to perform the impossible—to control extensive fires without vast supplies of water, their basic essential.

The fact that a largely inexperienced force of amateur fire-fighters faced and mastered the fires in the early weeks of the blitz with considerable success was in itself little short of a miracle. The 1939–40 lull allowed a great consolidation of training and equipment before the London raids effectively started; without this vital breathing space, it is unlikely that the small core of professional firemen of the LFB would have been able to cope unaided. If Hitler's wrath had not been channelled towards the Russian Front when it was, one can only speculate on what might have happened after the final assault of 10 May; after that massive raid, the LFS was literally on its knees, bowed but still wearily unyielding. Had the massed Luftwaffe squadrons of Air Fleet Two returned to London in the darkness of 11 May 1941, the direction of the war might well have been dramatically changed. Had another such raid occurred the next night, the capital would have undoubtedly been in danger of experiencing another and far more devastating Great Fire of London.

Perhaps a quotation from the diary of Samuel Pepys, recording the end of the Great Fire of 1666, is apt to apply to the end of both the blitz period and the months of sustained flying-bomb and rocket attacks: 'Up by five o'clock; and

blessed be to God! Find all's well!' As an epitaph to the hero-
ism of the men and women who were charged with the fire
defence of London during the Second World War, surely, no
finer parallel can be made.

Driven under nightmare
Of a disrupting star: exiled into dreams,
Spirit and flesh of nature:
Being fury-pursued, haunted
By throbbing net of high advancing steel
Wings: dive with me where
Beneath the ascendant doom which seems
Destructive in each downwards-pointing feature
By human will invented,
In your uttermost need my words may feel

Your agony, England!
Arise, rose of the blood,
Blaze from thorns of the heart!
Martyred blood of garlanded past days
Burn from the bombed and bitter island!
May your flesh petals torn to dust apart
By the blast of rays,
In burning beauty revive their flushed transparent good!

Covered with ashes is your statued past,
Once sunlit, where each soul his heritage
From-birth-to-death-span tilled, plotting deliberate choice
Of his willed good or evil flowers.
Destiny more glittering and vast
Than simple single sight fading through life to growing death
        and knowledge,
Blinds faith's towers.
Nor is there any voice,
Nor any bell to mourn the loss
Of that which died before . . .
The faith the stones are shaped to imitate,
Without whose fire beneath

Retrospect

Aspiring to the climax of the Cross,
The lion of rage is loosed to roar,
The once-caged Satan to create
The death of life, and then this life of death.

from 'Destruction and Resurrection—England Burning':
Stephen Spender (fireman, No 34 Fire Force, London)

Bibliography

The Battle of South London (Crystal Publications, 1945).

Blackstone, G. V. *A History of the British Fire Service* (Routledge & Kegan Paul, 1957).

Collier, Basil. *The Defence of the United Kingdom* (HMSO, 1957).

Collier, Richard. *The City that Wouldn't Die* (Collins, 1959).

Fire, (journals), various.

Fire and Water—an NFS Anthology (Lindsay Drummond, 1942).

Firebrace, Sir Aylmer. *Fire Service Memories* (Andrew Melrose, 1948).

Fire over London, London County Council, Hutchinson, 1941.

Flint, V. *The Bells Go Down* (Methuen, 1942).

From Debris to Nursery (NFS, 1945).

HMSO. *Front Line* (1942).

HMSO. *Roof over Britain* (1945).

Howard Roberts, J. R. *The National Fire Service* (1942).

In the Service of the Nation (NFS Benevolent Fund, 1944).

Jackson, W. Eric. *London's Fire Brigades* (Longman, 1966).

Jim Braidy. *The Story of Britain's Firemen* (Lindsay Drummond, 1943).

Kenyon, J. *Fourth Arm* (Harrap, 1948).

London Fire Brigade Library (various war diaries, reports and papers, 1938–1945).

London's Hour, LFS Benevolent Fund (Staples Books, 1942).

Mosley, L. *Backs to the Wall* (Weidenfeld & Nicolson, 1971).

Mosley, L. *London Under Fire, 1939–45* (Pan, 1972).

Richardson, M. L. *London's Burning* (Hale, 1941).

Stedman, H. W. *Battle of the Flames* (Jarrolds, 1943).

Wassey, M. *Ordeal by Fire* (Secker & Warburg, 1941).

Acknowledgements

Many people have been of great assistance to me in the preparation of this book and amongst these I would especially like to thank the following who served in either the London Fire Brigade, the Auxiliary Fire Service or the National Fire Service during the time covered by this work: R. 'Nobby' Clark, Mrs Peggy Jacobs (née Joseph), BEM, Harold Harvey, Jack Hoare, Frank Reader, Arthur Sullivan, CBE, and 'Mac' Young. The help of librarians of the Imperial War Museum; the Fire Service Staff College, Dorking; and the London Fire Brigade was of considerable value, as was that of the staff of the London Fire Brigade photographic section and Gordon White, LFB press officer. Adrian Falks aided me with much of the photographic processing.

I am indebted to Martin Secker & Warburg Ltd for permission to quote passages from Michael Wassey's *Ordeal by Fire* (1941) and to Methuen & Co Ltd for similar approval to quote from *The Bells Go Down* by V. Flint (1942). I also acknowledge the use of small extracts from *Fire Service Memories* (1948) by Sir Aylmer Firebrace, CBE (Andrew Melrose Ltd) and for some material from *Fire and Water* (1942), originally published by Lindsay Drummond Ltd. This latter work is an anthology by a number of serving firemen and women, and was in part responsible for the awakening of my interest in wartime fire service matters. Amongst the contributors to *Fire and Water*, I am particularly grateful to Stephen Spender, CBE for his kind permission to quote some of his wartime poetry, and for an account of life in a wartime London fire station.

Lastly, I wish to thank my wife Sue who has typed the MS with an indefatigable spirit and who gave me great encouragement throughout the research and completion of the book.

Index

Numbers in *italics* refer to illustrations.

Index